Finding Corporate Resources

Finding Corporate Resources

Maximizing School/Business Partnerships

Gayle Jasso

CORWIN PRESS, INC.
A Sage Publications Company
Thousand Oaks, California

For information address:

Corwin Press, Inc.
A Sage Publications Company
2455 Teller Road
Thousand Oaks, California 91320
e-mail: order@corwin.sagepub.com

SAGE Publications Ltd.
6 Bonhill Street
London EC2A 4PU
United Kingdom

SAGE Publications India Pvt. Ltd.
M-32 Market
Greater Kailash I
New Delhi 110 048 India

Printed in the United States of America

Library of Congress Cataloging-in-Publication Data

Jasso, Gayle.
    Finding corporate resources : maximizing school/business
partnerships / Gayle Jasso.
        p.   cm.
    Includes bibliographical references.
    ISBN 0-8039-6450-1 (alk. paper). — ISBN 0-8039-6451-X (pbk. :
(alk. paper)
    1. Industry and education—United States. 2. Education—United
States—Finance. I. Title.
LC1085.2.J37   1996
370.19'316—dc20   95-53345

This book is printed on acid-free paper.

96 97 98 99 00 10 9 8 7 6 5 4 3 2 1

Corwin Press Production Editor: S. Marlene Head

Contents

Acknowledgments

This book could not have been written without the leadership and friendship of Wayne Carlson. I've heard many of his friends call him "The Guru of Partnerships." Wayne taught me the value of a symbiotic relationship between peers and between institutions, especially important when the education and preparation of our youth are at stake. He demonstrated to me the meaning of the words "gentleman" and "professional." Never pushy, always considerate, always concerned for students, for my personal situation within my corporation, and for my corporation's situations and concerns, he taught, encouraged, and empowered me to "work" my system, one of America's largest banking institutions, for the benefit of the community and his school district. Prior to a well-earned retirement, Wayne served students as an administrator and teacher in the Los Angeles Unified School District, the second largest school system in the United States. For more than 15 years, as each of our careers blossomed largely in part because of what we accomplished as corporate and school partners, he helped me to see not "what is" but "what is possible." I saw and I believed.

GAYLE JASSO

About the Author

Gayle Jasso has served education for more than 25 years. In 1995, she joined Baldwin Park Unified School District's Adult School as the Grants Writer. She began teaching high school English in Utah and then taught 6 more years in California before becoming a public relations executive.

From 1976 through 1991, she rose to the position of First Vice President and Manager of Community Affairs for Security Pacific Corporation, the fifth largest U.S. bank holding company at the time of its merger with Bank of America in 1992.

While at Security Pacific, she created and managed more than a dozen programs that served communities in six western states. Her community relations responsibilities included special events management; public relations; and the creation, implementation, and management of programs. Her programs included job skills training programs, which annually trained more than 4,500 students, and corporate volunteer programs, which involved more than 5,000 employees and retirees in the community through more than 300 service projects each year. Her awards include President Reagan's 1986

Volunteer Action Award for Best Overall Corporate Effort, presented to her at the White House, and her public relations profession's highest award, the Silver Anvil.

In 1991, she left Security Pacific to form a consulting business with her husband. She has written five books and nine manuals that show individuals from corporations, nonprofit organizations, and schools how to apply public relations principles to enhance their organizations' reputations and their own careers.

She has earned an M.A. in English from CSU, Los Angeles, and a Professional Designation in Public Relations from UCLA. She resides in Altadena, California, with her husband Drake, her son David, and four Cavalier King Charles Spaniels.

*This book is dedicated
to my husband Drake
and to Lucky,
my first Cavalier King Charles Spaniel.
In their own special ways,
they taught me
not to give up too soon.*

Introduction

A Multifaceted Career

I have had the good fortune to have a successful, varied, and multifaceted career. While in college, I fell in love with English, so naturally I became a high school English teacher. Then I wanted to see what else was out there for me in the real world. My quest for my "dream job" was made prior to the resources of career education and career centers, but at last I discovered public relations, a profession much like teaching English because both fields require the same fundamental skills of writing, communicating, and planning.

My first PR job was in the insurance and financial services industry. I struggled to write copy and material addressing issues of interest to the readers who were experts in those fields. I asked my boss, "How am I supposed to know what to write?" He yelled, "You study until you know as much as they do."

Well, I really didn't care a whole lot about insurance and financial services. What I knew and cared a lot about was education, so I began searching for a job that would enable me to combine my new-found career, which I loved, with content, which I knew and cared about. That decision led me directly to my dream job.

A Nonbanker Banker

For 15 years, I worked for Security Pacific Corporation, which became the fifth largest U.S. bank holding company prior to merging with Bank of America. I spent those 15 years as a nonbanker, starting out as an officer and the Director of Educational Relations. My job was to work with the schools throughout California to help them in the areas that made sense for the bank. In those days, those areas were career and vocational education.

Step by step, a piece at a time, I created, implemented, and managed programs that touched the lives of more than 4,500 students each year from more than 200 California school districts. More than 3,500 of those students came into Security Pacific offices around the state to learn more than 15 entry-level jobs. Their classes were taught on bank premises; used state-of-the-art bank equipment, procedures, and materials; and were taught by bank employees who were qualified to be, and completed the necessary course work to become, credentialed teachers. They were then hired by the school districts as part-time teachers. I had a "faculty" of more than 50 teachers, each of whom was a professional banker or businessperson in his or her area of interest and expertise and who absolutely loved teaching students.

All of these corporate resources were provided *free* to the schools by my employer, who was pleased and proud to provide these things because of the terms "corporate citizenship" and "enlightened self- interest," ideas you will be mastering as you read this book. This advanced educational concept originated with the Los Angeles Unified School District. It worked so well with them that I took the idea around the state and "sold" it to other districts. Some "bought" it and some didn't—for lots of reasons—including the fact that many were threatened by it. And that's how I learned firsthand about business and education relationships, long before the term "partnerships" was coined and became popular.

These programs ultimately brought me recognition within my own corporation as well as within the state and the nation, including being honored by President Reagan at the White House. My responsibilities grew to include a corporate volunteer program, which I also created, implemented, and managed. It eventually involved more than 5,000 bank employees and retirees in six western states in their communities as volunteers. They provided service to community organizations and schools on behalf of their employer on their own time. By the time I finished my career at the bank, I was a first vice president who wanted to become a writer.

A Writer and an Educator After All

I left Security Pacific in 1991, 1½ years prior to the merger with Bank of America. I spent the next 3 years writing down everything I learned in my real-world career that would benefit schools and nonprofit organizations. While I was at the bank, I often felt like a double agent, because while serving my corporation and making it look and be good in the community, I was also channeling its resources out to the community with its full permission.

This unique experience is the basis for this book, which will provide inside knowledge and insights about how to find, get, and use corporate resources. Much of the information in this book is not even known or realized by most corporate executives and managers, so you will be ahead of the game as you work with them to achieve your goals.

This book will benefit school and college administrators, educational program coordinators, partnership and school volunteer coordinators, and innovative teachers who want to "get real" with their students and get more resources into their classrooms for their students.

The information in this book is fundamental to the major national movements of educational change and reform, including the Career Education Movement, the Partnership Movement, the Goals 2000 Movement, the School to Work/Career Movement, and the Integrated Curriculum (Academic and Career) Movement.

I have now come home to education, where I have been making a living using my writing skills. I couldn't be happier. While you are learning the information provided in this book, I will be surfing the Internet, searching for sources of grants and applying the same techniques I've written for you to procure corporate resources for education.

If you master what this book will teach you, and if I learn the ins and outs of grantwriting and practice what I have preached, together we will continue to bring badly needed outside resources to education, and we each will be able to sleep well at night knowing that we have made an important difference.

I

OPERATING IN THE CORPORATE ARENA

1

Taking the Mystery
Out of Corporations

A Corporate Stereotype

Corporations are typically stereotyped as huge, mysterious, and complex institutions housed in tall, intimidating steel and glass towers, headed up by ruthless corporate leaders focused on profits at any cost. This stereotype is frightening and intimidating to the people inside as well as outside of corporations. Like most stereotypes, it is usually not true.

Reality

Corporations are actually legal agreements that exist on paper, created by people to accomplish personal goals in accordance with current laws and customs. Once the legal documents have been drawn, symbiotic relationships must be formed between each corporate entity and the people involved with it. Corporations are owned in whole or in part by individuals called shareholders, who do not necessarily participate in the operation of the corporations.

Some people serve as members of a board of directors, providing management skills, expertise, and leadership, often in return for monetary reward, power, and influence. Some people serve as employees, providing talents, abilities, skills, and time in return for salaries and benefits such as insurance, savings, and retirement. Other people decide that they want to own or use the corporation's products and services. These people become a corporation's customers and clients.

The Good, the Bad, and the Ugly

Corporations are like people. Some corporations are good. Good corporations know why they exist and accomplish their goals with style. Some good corporations succeed, and some fail. Some corporations are bad. Many bad corporations lose their way, struggle to survive, fail, and disappear altogether, whereas some thrive. Some corporations are very definitely ugly, in their looks as well as their behavior.

People are the reason for the wide range of variation among corporations. Understand human nature, and you understand corporations. Some people are worth getting to know; some definitely are not! Some corporations are worth the time and effort required to establish meaningful, beneficial relations; some definitely are not!

Corporate Resources

Each corporation is a giant resource composed of many smaller resources used on behalf of the corporation and its affiliates. Some of these resources also can be used by community organizations and schools. Everything in this book is designed to teach you how to procure corporate resources for your educational institution. This book will actually teach you things about corporations that many corporations do not understand about themselves.

Most corporations, like most people, are so focused on daily survival that they do not realize the amount of good they can do if they just try. Many corporations are unaware of the wide range of resources that they have, *in addition to money,* that can significantly help people and institutions *without harming or weakening their own organizations.*

This book will take the mystery out of corporations by providing you with a better understanding and appreciation of how business executives think and how corporations operate, and by showing you how to procure the 12 types of corporate resources for your school.

Understanding corporations will enable you to help corporations become successful, contributing corporate citizens within their communities and enable your school to share in the profits of the corporations that serve your community.

Expectations

Just like people, not all corporations give away their resources. Some corporations give away their resources because (a) they believe they should help the community, (b) they are able to do so, and (c) they want to. Some corporations don't give away their resources because (a) they believe they should not help the community, (b) they are unable to do so, or (c) they don't want to.

Once you have discovered which corporations will be most likely to share their profits with your institution, avoid the others. It is wise to be "hopefully realistic" regarding the number of corporations that will help you and the amount of assistance they will provide.

Types of Relationships

When considering corporations as possible supporters, school administrators must decide what kind of relationships they want to have and maintain with corporations. Just like personal relationships, schools and corporations have individual reasons for being involved with one another, and the success of each relationship is based on understanding and respect.

Informal Relationships

There are three types of informal relationships between corporations and educational institutions:

1. *Casual introduction:* In this type of relationship, representatives from two institutions are formally introduced or meet one another at

a function. The value of this type of relationship is that should a need arise for one institution to connect with the other, the representative from one will not have to make a cold call to the representative of the other. The introduction serves as a "door opener."

2. *Acquainted:* In this type of relationship, representatives from two institutions have known one another either professionally or personally over a period of time.

3. *Friendly:* A friendly relationship is an acquainted relationship enhanced by a mutual liking and respect for one another by each of the parties, based on history. Friendly relationships are usually on a first-name basis. A friendly relationship is personal, not institutional, and has no formal ties or official agreements. However, when one or both parties are acting *on behalf of an employer*, the relationship must be strictly institutional in order to remain professional and ethical.

Formal Relationships

There are four types of formal relationships between corporations and schools, and these relationships exist for functional reasons.

1. *Cosponsor:* In this relationship, institutions are equals with specific obligations to fulfill in order to accomplish a mutual purpose, such as sponsoring an event or project.

2. *Grantor-Recipient:* In this relationship, one of the institutions, usually the corporation, gives one or more resources to the other institution, usually the school. The relationship is based only on the recipient's obligation to use the resource(s) in the manner specified in the grant or gift. Recipients of these resources must reapply for future contributions.

3. *Adoption:* An adoption is an official undertaking having a specific beginning and an unspecified ending. In this relationship, the corporation (the giver) formally "adopts" a school (the receiver), usually through some kind of formalized program, in order to achieve certain goals. Adopt-a-School programs are very popular in the United States.

   To improve perceptions, many school districts have changed the name of their Adopt-a-School programs to "Partnership" programs; however, most of these types of partnerships are still based on a giver-receiver relationship.

4. *Partnership:* In this relationship, two or more institutions enter into an official partnership or joint venture, often but not always through a formalized program, to accomplish mutually agreed-upon goals. Each partner agrees to perform certain roles and accomplish specific objectives. Partnerships are formed because each partner believes that it can successfully accomplish more objectives by working together with the other partner(s) than by working independently. Partnerships are becoming popular in preparing grant applications in hopes of strengthening the possibilities of winning.

Corporate Citizenship

Why would a corporation want to extend its focus beyond its primary reason for existing and channel some of its time, effort, energy, and resources into community service? There are many reasons. Some of them are selfish, and some are not.

Regardless of type and purpose, a corporation that either develops an ongoing community service effort or participates in community service projects or events has taken two giant steps. The first step has moved the corporation away from performing only those actions that produce the desired financial (bottom-line) results. The second step has changed management's perceptions of the corporation's purpose, attitude, philosophy, and sense of responsibility. Corporations that take these two significant steps become less self-centered and more socially responsible.

Top Management Support

Most members of top management within socially responsible corporations realize and believe that in addition to the excellent execution of the latest and best management techniques plus the application of state-of-the-art technology, a corporation's ability to achieve its goals, accomplish its purposes, and survive also depends on the following two factors:

1. The health and success of the community from which vital material and human resources must be drawn

2. A community's perception of a corporation as being sincerely committed to the community through words as well as ongoing, meaningful deeds that really make a difference

Enlightened Self-Interest

Socially responsible corporations believe it is their civic duty as well as in their best interest to be involved corporate citizens within their communities. This belief is called "enlightened self-interest." The citizenship of good corporate citizens has been called "the human side of enterprise."

In socially aware (and hopefully socially responsible) corporations, citizenship often finds form through the establishment of departments with names such as public affairs, community affairs, and community relations. Many corporations also establish charitable foundations.

If a corporation decides to try to be a good corporate citizen, that decision is never an accident. The choice is always the result of high intention, sincere effort, intelligent direction, and skillful execution. It represents the wise choice of many alternatives.

Corporate Structure

A corporation can appear overwhelming to a school. Because huge and complex corporations are often overwhelming, even to their own employees, how is a school supposed to have any idea where or how to find corporate resources? Here are some suggestions for how corporations are organized.

Line versus Support

In a corporation, "the line" represents individuals and departments or functions that produce income and contribute to the bottom line (profits). Examples of line departments are marketing, sales, and retail.

Support functions represent any individuals and departments or functions that assist the corporation in operating and that support the line. Examples of support (or staff support) departments are human resources, personnel, and public relations. In financially difficult times, support functions are the first to be downsized or eliminated.

Centralized versus Decentralized

Some corporations are organized in a centralized manner, which means that general functions are brought together under one roof or in one geographic location to serve an entire corporation. For example, a centralized human resources department would provide all of the personnel and human resource services for an entire organization regardless of the geographic location of the other departments, divisions, and offices.

In a decentralized corporation, operations and support services are provided at local or regional offices.

How Resources Are Given to the Community

In a centralized corporation, the corporation's resources are often distributed through centralized departments or functions with names such as foundation, corporate contributions, community relations, community affairs, or public affairs. These departments are usually located at the corporation's headquarters. Requests for resources must be sent to the proper department in the city in which the corporation is headquartered, either by the school itself or by a local corporate representative on behalf of the school.

In a decentralized corporation, regional or local managers of corporate offices may have authority to distribute some of the corporation's resources to the community. Representatives of schools should first contact the manager of the local office nearest the school and ask the manager how to apply to receive corporate contributions. If the local manager does not have the authority or the resources to make a contribution to the institution, he or she will provide the name and contact information for the proper individual within the corporation.

Players

Here are some of the titles of the key players whose approval must be obtained before any corporate resources can be given to a school. Their support often must be earned before a meaningful, ongoing relationship can be established between the corporation and an educational institution.

Middle Management

Department or Division Manager

The department or division manager is the senior manager of the department that distributes corporate resources to the community.

Foundation President

The foundation president is the president of the nonprofit foundation established by the corporation to disburse corporate resources to nonprofit institutions that have a 501(C)3 tax-exempt designation, and to educational institutions if they are a part of the foundation's purpose and contribution objectives. Sometimes, the school also must have a 501(C)3 tax designation to be considered for a grant.

Top Management

The CEO

The chief executive officer (CEO) is the highest ranking officer in the corporation. The only entity this individual reports to is the corporation's board of directors.

The COO

The chief operating officer (COO) is the person who is usually the second in command under the CEO. The COO runs the daily operations of the company. Often, the CEO asks the COO to provide top management support to the community on behalf of the corporation and the CEO.

The President

The president is the person who heads up the entire corporation or who heads up one of the corporation's subsidiaries (companies owned by the main corporation or "holding company"). If the president of the corporation is also the CEO or the COO, that person's title is usually the President and Chief Executive Officer or the President and Chief Operating Officer.

The Chairman of the Board

The chairman of the board is the individual who heads the corporation's board of directors. This title can also be combined with one of the other key corporate titles, as explained above.

Clout

Obviously, a relationship between a corporation and a school has more clout and receives more internal support and enthusiasm within each institution if the CEO (or the chief administrator) of the educational institution has a strong and positive working relationship with one or more of the corporation's key senior officers, and the higher the better.

It is also desirable for the heads of the departments that have received corporate resources to maintain strong positive relationships with the senior officers of the departments or foundation that actually contributed the support.

Channels

All institutions operate according to channels (i.e., who reports to whom from the bottom of the organization up to the CEO). For political, support, and survival reasons, it is essential for schools to work through the appropriate channels within their own organizations as well as those within the corporations with which they have relationships.

2

Acquiring Savvy for the Corporate Experience

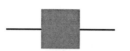

In Search of Volunteers:
How to Crack a Major Corporation

Does this sound familiar? You are the administrator of a nonprofit community organization. You have just returned from a marvelous national conference on volunteerism where you heard for days about wonderful corporations with hundreds of loving volunteers who are just dying to get

Author's Note: The key points I wish to make in this chapter are discussed thoroughly in an article that I wrote and had published in 1983. Although the article refers to volunteers and nonprofit organizations, the same principles apply to educational institutions regarding any corporate resource you may want to pursue. The Association of Volunteer Administration has graciously allowed me to share this article with you in its original form. Reprinted with permission from THE JOURNAL OF VOLUNTEER ADMINISTRATION, Vol I:4, Summer 1983, Association for Volunteer Administration.

involved in projects to help people. You walk into your office and sit down at your desk. Glancing about the jumbled room, you shake your head and wonder how you are ever going to get out from under all the paperwork, let alone conquer the great unknown of the mysterious and foreign corporate world.

But where do you begin? (That is the question.) And how do you do the job right? (That is the challenge.) For although you think you know nothing about "corporate types," your instincts tell you that, whatever you do, you had better not bungle the job because you will probably only have one chance to crack a major corporation.

As manager of community affairs for Security Pacific National Bank, I have been approached for years by representatives from numerous nonprofit organizations who have asked for help, be it financial support, requests for volunteers, or participation in any number of career and vocational education programs. My experience in dealing with these dedicated and well-meaning representatives of community organizations may be useful to you if you are the one responsible for mustering support in order to serve clients and keep your doors open. In this article, I've outlined key steps in attracting the support of corporations and have formulated 12 "rules" to guide you.

Play New Roles

After giving the matter much thought, I am convinced that a major corporation can be approached, then interested in and sold on a program and an organization if that organization's representative is willing to wear a few new hats and learn a few new skills to accomplish the job.

I believe successful nonprofit representatives must add the following new roles to their self-images and careers: detective, business executive, salesperson, and missionary. The latter role can only be successfully filled if the first three roles have already been effectively assimilated.

Why is being a detective first on your agenda? The reason is that you cannot sell a product if you do not have the *right buyer.* Ignoring this role leads to wheel spinning and burnout. Having doors slammed in your face does not do a lot for your ego. Playing detective in locating the right companies for you is essential to eliminate some of those slammed doors and open many others.

Use Contacts

Rule 1

The first and often most difficult rule to learn is to think in terms of contacts. From now on, every person you meet must be regarded as a contact who may be useful in the future. Scratch your head and try to remember anyone you have ever met or heard about who is connected to a business in your area. Friends, relatives, acquaintances, strangers who know someone you know—all must be considered. Any one of these people may be able to introduce you to someone, point you in the right direction, or open a door.

Rule 2

The second important rule is to swallow your pride and ask for help from these contacts. You may think your all-knowing and confident image will be shattered by admitting you need help, but usually it will not. In fact, asking for help makes you more human and makes others feel more comfortable around you.

Rule 3

Rule 3 is to follow the advice you receive, or at least look into it seriously. Nothing is so offensive as to ask for help or advice when you have no intention of using or following it. Your contacts soon learn not to waste their time and energy on you.

Rule 4

Rule 4 is to thank everyone who helps you. Send a special note, letter, or card as concrete evidence of thanks, and tell the person the results of his or her help and advice, especially if positive. Such a thoughtful touch will do much to further any relationship, and this is especially true with contacts.

Study the Corporation

Being a detective is essential when approaching a corporation. These factors must be considered:

1. Which corporation might be most likely to be supportive of your organization?
2. Whom in the company should you approach?
3. How should you approach this person?
4. What information will this person/corporation need to evaluate your request?

Question 1 will be answered by you through your research and contacts. Remember that a corporation's annual report provides lots of excellent information.

Question 2 is more challenging. Although corporate volunteer programs are becoming in vogue, most corporations do not have formal programs. Therefore, finding the appropriate department which has, should have, or could have such a program or involvement requires a private investigation that can usually be handled through a series of simple phone calls. Expect to be passed around within the company, but eventually you will find the right department with responsibility for the help you seek. Possible departments are public relations, community relations, community affairs, employee relations, or personnel. Every company is different.

Next you need to find the right person. By sticking with the secretary in the department you have located by perseverance, you can learn who approves requests for employee volunteers, how this person likes to be approached, and what information this person will need in order to be able to evaluate your request. At this point, thank the secretary very graciously and hang up. You will call back when you are wearing your salesperson hat.

Rule 5

Rule 5 is: Only sell to the person who can say "Yes."

Develop Your Personal Image

Before you contact the correct potential buyer in the corporation, you need to take a good look at your professional image and that of your organization. My advice is to think, look, and act like a business executive, because that is the type of person who can say "Yes" to your request.

If you are daring, take a deep breath and look at yourself in the mirror. Do you look like a professional businessperson, or do your clothes indicate a less formal occupation? Do you own a business suit (with a skirt for women)?

Rule 6

Rule 6 is to invest in yourself. Now is not the time to pat yourself on the back for being frugal and sacrificing. You need to pay the price to improve your image—not just for approaching corporations but in all of your professional endeavors.

Try it. Spend a little money on yourself. It will probably feel so good that you might decide to continue the investment. And remember, every professional must have a business card. If a card is not provided by your organization, print your own. You need to be able to leave a card with every contact, and in your new roles you will need plenty of cards as you meet all of those new contacts. Nothing spoils an impression like leaving someone your name, address, and phone number written on a scraggly piece of yellow lined paper.

Prepare Your Organization's Image

Can your organization present a professional image to the corporation? Does your organization have a proposal folder? Are your books in order? Do you have a current financial statement, list of board of directors, statement of purpose? These are things a corporation will probably require. If you walk into an interview well prepared, you will demonstrate that you and your organization could make effective use of that corporation's resources. Corporations are looking for winners—needy winners, but winners.

Realize That the Competition Is Stiff

I was offering comments such as these at a state conference on youth a few years ago, and many faces in the audience immediately turned hostile. One woman stood up and said that she resented having to put time and effort into a proposal package. She thought it was humiliating. After all, she was an educated professional. And besides, she could not afford good clothes on her salary. Her voice was shaking as she shared her thoughts.

Rule 7

My response was then and is now that this is life. The competition is stiff. Resources are limited. Those who receive help are those who make the best case for assistance in the most professional and well-prepared manner. Making this case includes how you look, what you say, how you say it, and the materials you present. These are the realities of life, not just of corporations. If you do not know how to act the part of the business executive, rule 7 should be helpful: Learn from role models. Learn from your new contacts.

Sell, Sell, Sell

Cracking a major corporation, or any business for that matter, boils down to selling. The first sales challenge is getting an interview. When you are granted an interview by *the right person*, you will have that one chance to sell yourself and your product, so the second sales challenge is persuading that individual to convince his or her corporation to assist your organization. You must convince this key person that by satisfying your organization's needs, the person will also be satisfying his or her company's needs.

My best recommendation is to take a seminar or read a book on sales techniques. Because getting a "Yes" answer is crucial, you will find the investment of time and money in such training and research well worthwhile. Such exposure will make you aware of various sales methods and stages such as qualifying, selling, and closing.

You will also need a supply of "ammunition" for your sales presentation. You must anticipate the person's questions, fears, and concerns and have good responses prepared. You will also need an impressive list of benefits to the corporation for helping your organization. The more specific the benefits, the better. For example, the benefit of increasing employee productivity is more specific than the possibility of creating goodwill or good public relations.

Consider every possible benefit to that corporation, and rank each in order of concrete payoff. A good brainstorming session with your peers could produce this valuable ammunition. If you have business friends, invite them to sit in. Their ideas will be helpful and give you more confidence in your list.

Rule 8

After you have presented your sales pitch, remember rule 8: Do not take "No" for an answer until you are sure it is absolutely, positively "No." In sales, "No" does not really mean "No." Often it is just the expression of another doubt or question which, with additional input of information or time, could become a "Yes."

Ask the Golden Question

Rule 9

Rule 9 is to ask what I call the "Golden Question." If you receive "No" for an answer, simply ask, "Well, what would I need to do to be able to get what I'm asking for?" Most often, the person will tell you exactly what your next steps should be. And if you follow this good advice, you are often on your way to a "Yes."

Rules 10 and 11

Rules 10 and 11 go hand in hand. Be persistent and be patient. Think of the time you spend with a corporation as an investment. If you have done your homework and carefully donned your roles as detective, business executive, and salesperson, the investment should pay off.

Demonstrate Commitment

At this point, we need to bring in the role of missionary. Actually, as a dedicated professional, you have probably always been an evangelist for your cause. The things to remember are to demonstrate dedication and commitment through your enthusiasm and joy in your work. These qualities will shine through your spirit, your eyes, your smile. This missionary role can often make the difference between a "Yes" and "No" answer. It can also make the difference between winning someone's support and turning someone off.

My recommendation is to aim at being a low-key, professional mission-ary. Such an approach can put the frosting on the cake. Too much eagerness will probably be counterproductive.

Remember that the missionary role should be in addition to the other important roles. Even if you are enthusiastic, without the groundwork of the other roles, you may not be taken seriously. You might make an impression, but not necessarily the one you had in mind.

Service the Account

My last piece of advice is to remember that the challenge really begins after making the sale and receiving the "Yes." Wearing your very best salesperson hat, please remember that although your goal is immediate, it should also be long-term. Think of the corporation as your account. You, your staff, and volunteers must provide ongoing and quality service to the account.

Corporations are composed of people who have feelings like everyone else. You can help corporations enjoy the sense of satisfaction that comes from being able to serve one's fellow citizens because, as we all know, helping people feels good. But businesspeople do not like to be taken advantage of, taken for granted, or taken for a ride. A little respect, consid-eration, and tender loving care will go a long way in cultivating meaningful, mutually beneficial relationships with corporations.

Enjoy the Relationship

Rule 12

There are thousands of corporations out there waiting to be "cracked." As you take on your new roles and apply the skills discussed here, I am confident you will find responsiveness from corporate towers. Remember, those towers are filled with human beings, potential volunteers, waiting to be given the opportunity to make a contribution to their communities. Your persistence and patience will enable them to feel good about themselves while you and your organizations better serve your clients. And that is the secret of the 12th and Golden Rule: Everyone must win.

3

Developing Corporate Outreach Skills

Determine Your Wants and Needs

With rare exception, most people and institutions, including corporations, want more than they have. Most people and institutions want more than they need. And most want, and at least think they need, more than they have the ability to acquire.

Because corporations are in the same boat, when schools ask corporations for assistance, two things are essential: (a) The school's wants or needs must be necessary, realistic, well thought out, and not wasteful; and (b) the school must have the sincere interest, ability, and determination to implement and use the things it wants and needs, if and when they are funded by a corporation.

Corporations and foundations are approached by far more people and organizations seeking assistance than they can possibly help. Therefore, funders use criteria to determine which community organizations and schools they will fund.

The following steps should be taken to help you determine your school's wants and needs.

Step 1

Decide what you want potential corporate supporters to do. The following questions will help you.

Question 1

How much money does each want or need require at an ideal or at least adequate level during a given calendar year (over and above the amount of budget allocations that will be provided by your school, if any)?

Question 2

Regarding the dollars needed beyond those being covered by your school, how will the money be used?

At this point you must be very specific and list the following:

1. Each and every item (described in detail)
2. The purpose for each item
3. The source of each item
4. The exact quantities required during the calendar year in question
5. The unit cost per item
6. The total cost per item, including tax and delivery
7. The total amount of dollars that must be raised from corporate supporters
8. The total amount of dollars that will be provided by your school
9. The total amount of dollars that will be provided by any other source
10. The methods you will use to fund these needs after the grants run out

Step 2

Separate the items needed and their costs into units that have nice round numbers. Each unit, or a combination thereof, can be funded by one or more corporate supporters.

Step 3

Establish goals for the number of corporate supporters you want to obtain and how much money and what resources each will contribute. For example, one single supporter could sponsor all of the units, or one supporter could sponsor each unit or a group of units.

Compare Your Dreams to Reality

Now that you have prepared yourself by developing a detailed projection of your school's wants and needs, you are ready to discover if your dream list can become a reality through corporate assistance.

Discover What They've Got

When most schools think about corporate resources, they usually think about money. In any economy, but especially in a down or flat economy, most corporations are as short of money as most people are.

This may come as a pleasant surprise to you as well as to the corporations themselves: Corporations have 11 other resources in addition to money that can help schools. Part II of this book presents a discussion of the 12 corporate resources, an example of how each resource may be able to help a school, and the pros and cons of each resource from a corporation's as well as a school's point of view.

By understanding the types of resources corporations have, your school can have a better idea of how the corporations in your community might be able to help your school meet its needs.

Mix and Match

Not every corporation will be able to provide all 12 resources, either because they do not have them or they cannot provide them. By analyzing the corporations within your community, you can decide which ones might have the best chances of providing the resources your school needs. Hopefully, by mixing and matching your school's needs with the various resources from the corporations in your community, you can procure enough resources to enable your school to achieve its goals, objectives, and dreams.

Learn Selling Skills

To implement any idea, the idea first must be accepted by the person who has the desire, power, and authority to implement it. If you want to receive corporate support, you're going to have to learn how to sell. Selling includes the process of presenting the idea to a potential "buyer," explaining the benefits of the idea, answering questions about the idea, and overcoming objections about the idea.

Leads

Each specific need for which funds must be procured must be sold to a corporation in the same professional manner in which a salesperson would sell a product to a corporation. For the purpose of this discussion, your funding need will be referred to as your "project."

To find the correct individual within the right corporation or foundation, you must develop leads. There are seven steps to follow in the process of developing leads for the corporations and foundations that may be able to provide resources to fund or support your project.

Step 1: School Contacts

Talk with the following people within your school and school district, and others within your organization who may be of assistance, and ask them for suggestions about corporations or foundations with which your organization already has relationships and that might be good candidates for becoming supporters of your school:

1. The principal
2. The assistant principals
3. The partnership coordinator
4. The school volunteer coordinator
5. The job placement and career counselors
6. The purchasing coordinator for your school and district
7. The grantwriters
8. The public relations coordinator
9. Your district's controller or business director

10. The executive director of your school district's foundation (if it has one)

Note: If the project is not currently being funded completely or partially by your district's own foundation, you must consider your own foundation as a major lead that could become one of your most important supporters. Follow all of the steps presented throughout the remainder of this chapter when communicating and meeting with the head of your district's foundation. If your foundation does become a supporter of your project, the foundation should be treated in the same manner as all other supporters and should receive the same appreciation and publicity for its contributions.

Step 2: Personal Contacts

Conduct the same kind of research that you conducted in Step 1, using your own personal external contacts and the external contacts recommended by anyone else.

Step 3: Prospects List

Develop a list of potential prospects. Find out who the CEO and the head of the foundation of each of these organizations are and obtain their correct names, titles, phone numbers, and addresses.

Step 4: School/District Approval

Find out who within your school and district must clear or approve of your contacting the individuals and organizations on your list.

Step 5: Necessary Approvals

For your sake politically, be sure to receive all necessary approvals from within your organization, including and especially your boss, before you contact any of the people from the organizations on your list.

Step 6: Presentation Development

Develop a presentation and practice it before you contact or visit anyone on your list.

Step 7: Calendar Appointments

Make appointments for yourself and whomever else should be included in the presentations of your project to corporations and foundations.

Create Your Presentation

Preparation

Abe Lincoln reportedly said that if he had 10 hours to cut down a tree, he would always take 9 hours to sharpen his axe! In making a sales presentation, the most important time you can spend is the time you spend preparing.

Step 1: Determine Features

Develop a brief, workable list of your project's (your school's needs that require funding or support) key features (the things that set your project apart from other needs and make it special and unique).

Step 2: Determine Benefits

Develop a brief, workable list of benefits that a corporation will receive as a result of funding or supporting your project. Benefits include

1. Helping the corporation achieve its goals and objectives
2. Being a good corporate citizen
3. Helping improve the quality of life for residents of the community
4. Receiving the appreciation of your school
5. Receiving positive public relations

Step 3: Determine Reasons

Develop a compelling case for support. The reasons should be meaningful, tangible, and important.

Step 4: Develop an Outline

Write an outline for your presentation, including the ideas developed in the first three steps above. Writing your outline yourself is important because you will feel most comfortable with and confident about the ideas when they are your own.

Step 5: Establish Belief

Be sure that you have a true belief in the value and importance of your project. This belief will be seen by each person with whom you meet.

Step 6: Prepare Answers

Be sure that you can explain and answer questions about your project and its many benefits without having to look at any notes.

Step 7: Memorize the Benefits

Memorize the benefits that the corporation will receive if it supports your project.

Step 8: Visualize the Presentation

Visualize the outline of your presentation from the beginning to the end. Memorize the key ideas of your presentation in the order that you think they should be presented, realizing that your presentation will key off from the comments of each corporate representative (prospect). You will need to be comfortable enough with your material to be able to present its components at the most effective and logical times during your presentation. It is not necessary and, in fact, not desirable to memorize the entire presentation word for word because you don't want to look like you have been programmed. Your presentation and comments must be informal and comfortable for both you and the prospect.

Step 9: Develop an Introduction

Develop a comfortable introduction of yourself and anyone else who will be accompanying you.

Step 10: Ask for the Help

Develop a comfortable way to ask the corporation for the support you want in a positive, confident manner.

Step 11: Follow Up

Be prepared to follow up as often as necessary after the initial presentation until you either receive the support you want or are absolutely, positively told "No" (and maybe not even then, because every good salesperson knows that "No" does not definitely mean "No").

Step 12: Practice!

Presentation Goals

Goal 1

Your first goal is to have each prospect and his or her corporation become a supporter or sponsor of your project, preferably now, but if not now, certainly in the future.

Goal 2

Your second goal is to have each prospect and his or her corporation become a "friend" of yours, your school, and your project, regardless of whether or not the corporation becomes a sponsor or supporter of your project at this time.

Understand the Sales Presentation

Selling is an art that requires knowledge, skills, practice, experimentation, and just the right cultivation of ingredients that best suit the personality, style, and temperament of each individual salesperson. According to Percy H. Whiting in *The Five Great Rules of Selling,* a good sales presentation has five steps.

Step 1: Attention

You have to get the prospect's attention and make sure he or she is listening to you or else you can't sell the prospect.

Step 2: Interest

Once you have the prospect's attention, you have to keep it by creating and sustaining an interest in what you are saying.

Step 3: Conviction

You must convince your prospect that it will be a wise and good thing to do what you have asked him or her to do—to buy your product, which means to support or sponsor your project.

Step 4: Desire

You must create within the prospect a desire for what you are selling, and so strong a desire that he or she will want to satisfy that desire.

Step 5: Close

You must help the prospect make his or her decision to buy your product. You help him or her make that decision through an effective close. The two parts of the act of closing a sale are getting the decision and getting the approval or signature.

Keep It Short and Simple

Your sales presentation must be boiled down to a short, concise, interesting presentation. Carefully watch your prospect and be sure he or she is not becoming bored. If you see that he or she is, immediately change your approach and move on in the presentation. Don't complete your entire, fully envisioned and prepared presentation at the expense of losing the sale.

Resources

If you are interested in increasing your knowledge and understanding of the art of selling, the following books are excellent resources:

Dove, Kent E. (1988). *Conducting a successful capital campaign: A comprehensive fundraising guide for nonprofit organizations.* San Francisco: Jossey-Bass.

Johnson, Spencer, & Wilson, Larry. (1984). *The one-minute salesperson.* New York: William Morrow.

Whiting, Percy H. (1979). *The five great rules of selling.* New York: Dale Carnegie & Associates.

Find Out What They'll Give

There are two major methods of discovering what resources a corporation has that could be made available to your school. Each method can result in success, and each requires you to make a personal contact and establish an appropriate relationship with the key person responsible for making contributions and support decisions.

The Specific Request Method

In this method, your school can define its specific wishes and needs and then ask a corporation if it will provide them. If the corporation says "Yes," you have your answer. If it declines your request, you have two options: (a) Ask the corporation if it will fund a different project or (b) move on to a new corporation. This method works best if your school already has established a strong relationship with the chosen corporation, such as a partnership or an adoption.

The Research Method

This method consists of three steps.

Step 1: Study

Before you submit a request for support to a corporation, study the corporations that would most likely have the ability and the desire to support you. (The desire would be based on their motives and needs for becoming involved with your school.)

One of the best ways to conduct the necessary research is to request a copy of a corporation's annual report and its contributions or community service report, which are often combined in the same document. If a corporation has a separate charitable foundation, the foundation will have its own annual report that usually includes very specific guidelines for submitting grant requests. These guidelines must be followed to the letter!

Step 2: Use Leads

After you have acquired and studied the corporate information, compare the results with the leads information you have developed. If you have not yet begun to develop your leads, follow the instructions previously provided in this chapter. The strongest corporate candidates will be those corporations that rank highest after you combine the research data with your leads and contacts information. This ranking will tell you which corporations to approach first.

Step 3: Conduct Interviews

The next step includes contacting the person at each corporation who has the authority to grant your wish and interviewing him or her either in person or by phone. Using the Corporate and Foundation Resources Worksheet (Appendix A) found at the end of this book, go over the list of the 12 corporate resources and find out which ones the corporation has that it could possibly make available to your school. If the person you contact is not sure exactly what a specific corporate resource is or how it could be used by your school, use the examples of resources listed on your form along with the information included in Part II of this book regarding each of the 12 corporate resources.

Now you have enough information about each corporation and the resources it might be able to make available to your school to develop a realistic action plan. Analyze the overall corporate resources and compare them with your school's wants and needs list. Then determine which corporations to ask for what resources. Persist until you have achieved your school's goals, objectives, and dreams.

Developing successful, ongoing relationships with corporations requires a system for recording all major interaction and results. A good system will enable your school to have an accurate, up-to-date record of the activity and results of each corporate relationship. Such a record will enable your school to know which people from your school, and hopefully from the district office, have had interaction with each corporation, enabling your school to know "what the right and left hands are doing."

4

Administering
Corporate Relationships

Cultivating and Sustaining Relationships

Effort and Style

The goal of every school/business relationship must be that it is strong, positive, supportive, mutually respectful, and ongoing. In addition to positive community relations, a primary reason for your school to develop quality relationships with corporations and their foundations is the hope that future contributions of resources will be received. In this chapter, each aspect of your school that needs corporate support will be referred to as "your project."

The effort required, be it in person or by mail, to cultivate and sustain positive and effective business relationships must be perceived as and believed to be worth the effort by the school's key administrators and those who will be directly involved with the companies. Anyone who has any dealings

35

with any corporate supporter must demonstrate professionalism, compe-
tence, appreciation, and respect.

School Representative

As you are trying to decide who will be the right person to represent your
project and your school to each corporation or business, keep these two
questions in mind: (a) Who is the most appropriate person who will have the
time and take the time needed to do a good job? (b) Who will do the best job
of developing and sustaining quality relationships between our school and
each business supporter?

Information

Members of your district's school board and your district's and school's
senior administrators, along with each corporate sponsor's board of directors
and top management, will be more inclined to provide ongoing support to
you and your project if you and anyone involved with the project do two
important things: (a) Show these important people what the project is all
about; and (b) show them how the project benefits your school and the
company (if possible), and how the project serves your school's and the
company's clients and the community.

In addition to making reports in person at board and management or
administrative meetings, other vehicles for providing information are copies
of current project reports and newsletters, and information about upcoming,
exciting, and important project-related events.

Enthusiasm

It is important that the coordinators of your project and anyone involved
with it maintain and exhibit enthusiasm about the project and its potential
accomplishments for your school. Enthusiasm is contagious.

Invite Them

Members of your school board and senior administration, along with
members of each corporate sponsor's board of directors and senior manage-

ment, should be invited to attend large, highly visible, especially important, and fun project-related or school-sponsored events. Involving these key leaders in simple but ongoing ways will help them to understand and appreciate your project and your school.

Appreciate Them

Everyone needs to feel appreciated, even and especially board members and members of an organization's senior management. Whenever board members, high-level administrators, or members of a company's senior management attend or participate in a project-related or school-sponsored event, the school coordinator in charge should do two important things: (a) Provide a personal school host for *each* corporate representative during the event, and (b) write these important people thank-you notes *immediately* after the event. A gift of a project promotional or recognition item is another special and tangible way of saying "Thank you for your support!"

Recognition and Publicity

Recognition

Immediately after your school receives a grant or gift of a resource from a corporation or its foundation, a letter from your institution's CEO (the superintendent or the principal) should be written to the appropriate person, preferably the corporation's CEO or the president of its foundation, with a copy of the letter going to your primary contact at the corporation. The letter should express appreciation for the grant or support and give assurance that the corporation's support and resources will be well used.

It is recommended that a tangible thank-you gift, such as an award or a promotional item, be presented to your primary contact at the corporation. The gift should be presented, with each recipient's full knowledge and approval, at a well-chosen time and place when and where the direct recipient and his or her corporation will receive the greatest amount of benefit and recognition.

Publicity

You and your primary contact at the corporation must make decisions regarding the type of publicity that will be released about the corporation's involvement with or support of your institution and the proposed publications to which this news will be submitted.

External News Releases

The goal of your institution must be to ensure that the exact type, wording, and amount of external publicity occurs and is completely satisfactory to each corporation or its foundation that supports your school. Sometimes, a corporation is more comfortable having news about its grant or sponsorship come from your institution than from itself so that the public will not think that the corporation is bragging. Sometimes, a corporation prefers to release all information regarding its organization through its own public relations experts. Sometimes, a corporation wants as much publicity as possible from every possible source. And sometimes, a corporation wants no publicity at all.

Internal News Releases

Each corporate sponsor will probably want to handle the release of information about its contribution to your school in its own way through its own internal communications vehicles. Any release of information, along with the exact words to be used, about the company's contribution within your own district or school also must be approved by the corporation *prior to* publication.

These precautions will ensure that the corporation approves of each announcement in principle and is completely satisfied with the words, the communication vehicles, and the purposes for each announcement.

Use of the Corporation's Name and Logo

Any proposed use of the corporation's name and logo by your institution must be approved by your primary contact at the corporation. If other corporate approval is required, your contact will receive approvals from all necessary corporate people. It is recommended that, if approved, the corporation's name and logo be used on all promotional and informational materials regarding each project supported by the corporation.

The Value of Win-Win

Kinds of Relationships

In any relationship, be it between people or organizations, the same basic principles apply. If people and organizations are able to work together and meet their needs through a relationship, those involved will be far more likely to continue the relationship.

There are three basic kinds of school/business relationships.

Win-Lose Relationships

If one organization wins and the other loses, the winner may win the battle, but more than likely it will lose the war. Even if the loser feels happy for the winner because it won something that it wanted, the loser may feel bad about the relationship, especially if the loser is not receiving what it needs from the relationship. If one organization's winning causes the other organization to lose something it really wants, sooner or later the loser will feel so bad about the relationship and the other organization that it will end the relationship.

Lose-Lose Relationships

If both organizations lose things that they really want as a result of their relationship with one another, it will not take long before the key contacts and members of top management from each organization begin to evaluate the degree or lack of success and the perceived and actual cost of the relationship. If a lose-lose relationship is wasting a corporation's time and resources, the corporation may take necessary steps to end the relationship regardless of the political and public relations ramifications, especially if the corporation is experiencing financial difficulties.

Win-Win Relationships

The ideal relationship is a "win-win" relationship, meaning that both organizations win at least something that each values. Because each organization feels good about the end results and the costs of their relationship with one another, the relationship has a much greater chance of continuing. Therefore, the receiver (usually the school) must do everything possible to ensure that the giver (usually the corporation) achieves its desired goals for being involved in the relationship.

Value-Added Benefits

Following are some examples of some value-added benefits that can be provided by the receiver (more than likely the school) to the giver (more than likely the corporation) in order to cultivate and enrich a school/business relationship:

1. Prompt, sincere, tangible, personalized symbols of gratitude from the direct recipients of the resources, such as thank-you letters, recognition items, or promotional items representing the receiving organization

2. Prompt, sincere acknowledgment of the gift or support, expressed through the personal gratitude, interest, and respect of the receiving organization to the key contacts within the giving organization

3. Publicity developed and placed in the media by the receiving organization, with the full approval of the necessary parties from the giving organization (enabling the giving organization to receive public credit and recognition for its generosity without having to arrange for it itself and appear to be bragging)

4. An offer to share some of the receiving organization's resources with the giving organization, such as meeting rooms, eating facilities, and parking, if such offers are legal and appropriate

5. Enabling the giver to use the receiver's lobbyists to help provide support on issues of mutual benefit to both organizations, if such use is legal

6. Providing support and expertise from the receiver to facilitate a project or event sponsored by the giver, such as speechwriters and facilitating staff

7. Utilization, as customers, of the giver's products or services
8. Representation of the giver in leadership positions within the receiver's organization, if such representation is legal and does not represent a conflict of interest
9. Referrals for possible clients for the giver by the receiver
10. Introductions and access for the giver to key people known by the receiver

Win-Win-Win

Organizational relationships are obviously far more complex than are relationships between individuals. Organizational relationships are based on the skills, savvy, feelings, and perceived level of satisfaction of the individuals who represent each organization as well as of their superiors.

An excellent way to ensure that a school/business relationship succeeds is to make sure that in addition to satisfying the main coordinators and their superiors, the relationship also benefits each organization's key clients. When each organization benefits *and* the clients benefit, the result will be a win-win-win relationship. When everyone wins, relationships can survive changes in players, power, and economics.

Developing Relationship Management Systems

The coordination of corporate relationships is usually added to the duties of someone within the district or school who is already working to capacity. Occasionally, often in very large districts that have or intend to have many corporate relationships, one person will be assigned "just" to coordinate these important relationships. Either way, corporate relationships must receive priority attention for all of the reasons explained throughout this book and especially in this chapter.

School/corporate relationships must be well organized, efficient, and effective. A school's or district's right hand must indeed know what the left hand is doing when it comes to corporations. Business executives do not have time to be contacted by different representatives of an educational institution and asked for different or even the same items.

Each and every *contact* with each and every company, and each and every *contribution* must be logged, monitored, and "managed" by the business relationship coordinator. Careful logging and record keeping are the only ways to ensure that corporations receive well-organized, prompt, and appropriate contact by schools. The Relationship Record (Appendix B) and Contributions Record (Appendix C) found at the end of this book will serve as a starting point for you to coordinate your corporate relationships.

II

MASTERING THE 12
CORPORATE RESOURCES

How to Use Part II

Understanding the 12 Corporate Resources

This section will explain the kinds of resources corporations have that can be made available to the community and to your school if the corporations are willing and able to contribute them. The corporate resources are presented in alphabetical order. Remember, most business executives do not even realize that their businesses have all of these resources that can be very useful to schools.

By studying each of the 12 corporate resources, you will have a keen understanding of what corporations have so that you can compare it to what your school wants and needs. Then, by applying what you learned from reading Part I of this book, you will be able to help the executives *want* to help your school.

Chapter Sections

To help you fully understand and analyze each corporate resource, where appropriate, each of the following 12 chapters is presented in 10 major sections.

Section 1: Sample Challenge

This section presents a specific example of a challenge that is facing a school. As you read the example, try to think of similar situations that currently exist or have existed at your school and within your school district.

Section 2: Possible Outreach Solution

This section explains how a school administrator or project coordinator could solve his or her problem or challenge by reaching out to a corporation and asking for help. An example is provided of what a corporation could give to the school that is described in Section 1. The corporate contribution would solve the school administrator's problem or challenge and enable the school to achieve its objectives.

Section 3: Resource Description

This section provides background and discussion regarding the corporate resource to help you understand the resource and how you could apply it to the needs of your school.

Section 4: Explanation of the Corporate Resource

This section gives a simple, basic explanation of the corporate resource from the corporation's perspective (e.g., what the corporation has that it could contribute to schools).

Section 5: Source of the Corporate Resource

This section explains exactly where the resource comes from. It is easy to understand that material resources come from the corporation; however, when it comes to employees and retirees, who "belong" to the corporation because of their relationship with the company as employees and retirees, a distinction must be made as to whether the contribution is actually a gift from the corporation, or whether it is from the employees and retirees themselves but made possible through the efforts of their corporation.

Section 6: Examples of the Resource

This section presents five specific examples of the corporate resource that could be used by a school.

Sections 7 and 8: Pros and Cons—Corporations

As with most things in life, there are pros and cons. These two sections explain, from the corporation's perspective, the pros and cons of providing the specific corporate resource to a school. This information is invaluable in helping you understand where a corporation is coming from in its decisions and actions. It is hoped that the information will also result in the development of empathy on the part of educators for businesspeople and the decisions they must make to remain in business.

Sections 9 and 10: Pros and Cons—Schools

As with any "gift," there may be obligations or strings attached. These sections will help a school understand the pluses and minuses of accepting this particular corporate resource. If a school administrator decides that the cons are not worth the pros, then he or she should decline the contribution but work toward maintaining and strengthening the relationship.

5

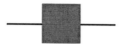

Corporate Resource No. 1:
Events

Sample Challenge

The principal of an adult and continuation education program of a unified school district wishes to sponsor a walkathon to raise money for an after-school day care and teen parent education program for disadvantaged youth. Her school board approved the walkathon but instructed her not to spend any school funds on the event.

Possible Outreach Solution

The principal can ask one or more corporations to sponsor and fund all or part of the event in return for publicity as "the" or "a" corporate sponsor and positioning as one of the leading corporate citizens in the community.

Special Events

Like the definition of a short story, an event is an activity that has a beginning, a middle, and an end. In public relations jargon, this type of an activity is called a *special event*. A special event has four major phases: planning, implementation, follow-up, and evaluation.

The amount of time and effort required to plan a special event depends on factors such as the degree of complication, the perceived significance by members of top management and the administration, the number and importance of the people who will be invited to attend and those who will participate in the program as speakers and entertainers, and the cost.

Special events management is a profession unto itself. These professionals are often called meeting planners. The ins and outs of special event management are thoroughly presented in my book called *Special Events From A to Z: The Complete Educator's Handbook,* also published by Corwin Press.

Resource Description

A corporation can sponsor (e.g., fund, staff, or both) special events either (a) independently, created by the corporation to achieve a community relations goal; or (b) created by one or more educational institutions with the goal of gaining full or shared corporate sponsorship to facilitate the event. Such events are intended to achieve the objectives of the originating school(s). Often, one of the primary purposes of such an event is to raise funds for a school.

Source of the Corporate Resource

Corporate

Corporate resources include funds, staff, administrative operations, in-kind services, and employees who are granted released time from work to help staff or participate in an event. The volunteer hours provided by the employees are actually a contribution of the corporation.

Employees and Retirees

A corporation's employees and retirees have a resource that they can give to schools—their *personal* volunteer time. For employees, this time must take place outside of work hours in order for the gift to be from them as individuals rather than from the corporation.

Examples of Special Events

1. An awards or recognition event (e.g., outstanding volunteers, students, community service, citizenship)
2. A celebration event (e.g., luncheon, reception, dinner, cultural event, holiday party, or festival)
3. A sporting event (e.g., golf tournament, track meet, race, the Special Olympics)
4. A fundraising event (e.g., telethon, auction, March of Dimes Walkathon, The Human Race)
5. A joint charities event where multiple agencies share the funds raised (e.g., San Diego's America's Finest City Week, and San Francisco's Bay to Breakers); the overall events are very large and complicated, often consisting of multiple events that occur throughout one or more days

Pros—Corporations

1. The corporation can be positioned as an involved corporate citizen among other corporations, including its competitors.
2. The corporation can handle a portion of the event, from small to total, depending on the corporation's reasons for sponsorship and the type and amount of resources it can and wants to contribute.
3. Events have a beginning and an end, and most require a relatively short-term commitment. After each event, the corporation can decide

whether or not to participate in the next one based on the event's success, the achievement of the corporation's and community organization's goals, and the availability of future corporate resources.

4. Events are excellent sources of positive media coverage.

5. The schools that are served often provide staff support to the corporate sponsors. Quality staff support is a benefit and takes some of the burden of time and effort from the shoulders of each corporate sponsor.

Cons—Corporations

1. Events can be very costly in terms of both money and staff time.

2. A corporation's participation in events that are not particularly unusual will not make a definitive and distinct impact within the community for the corporation.

3. Participation in an event may be perceived as a waste of corporate resources by senior management and shareholders, especially if there is little or no connection between the event and the corporation's purpose and goals.

4. It is often difficult to justify to schools the corporation's selection of one school's special event over another school's event.

5. It is easy and common for a corporation's community relations department to become hooked into a senior executive's pet event. Often, the community relations department must participate in a pet event without being provided with additional budget allocations. These internal political situations are challenging to community relations department staff members, who may have previously committed those same corporate funds to another community organization.

Pros—Schools

1. The corporation(s) may have more resources to devote to an event than does the school.

2. It is often easier to sell a corporation on sponsoring or cosponsoring an event (which has a beginning and an end) than it is an ongoing program or relationship.

3. Events are often publicized in the media, thus linking the school to the corporation and enhancing the school's perceived reputation (assuming the corporation has a positive public image).

4. It is easier for the involved staff members of the school to sustain interest, energy, and enthusiasm for an event than for an ongoing program.

5. The administrators and leaders of the school will more than likely have more authority and control over the event than the representatives of a corporation.

Cons—Schools

1. The corporation may ask the school to do all or most of the work.

2. A special event usually requires a significant amount of staff time and resources to plan and implement professionally and successfully.

3. If an event is of particular interest to a corporation, there may be pressure to continue doing the event in order to maintain the relationship with the corporation, when the school would prefer discontinuing the event.

4. Changes in the economy affect a corporation's interest in and ability to participate in an event.

5. Fundraising events often cost more money in terms of time and resources than the events are able to raise.

6

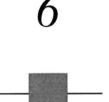

Corporate Resource No. 2: Human Resources

Sample Challenge

The principal of an elementary school is concerned about the reading and math levels of his fourth-grade students. There are no funds to provide additional classroom aides.

Possible Outreach Solution

The principal can approach the community's largest and oldest employer, preferably but not necessarily near the school. Because the principal believes that the employer will not want or be able to provide assistance from its employees because that would require taking some of them away from their jobs, he plans to request that some of the company's retirees and night-shift employees be asked to participate as volunteer tutors during school hours.

Human Beings—The Most Valuable Resource

As with any type of institution, a corporation's most valuable resources are its human resources. The employees and retirees of a corporation have a rainbow of skills, talents, and expertise, combined with their desires to help improve the quality of life and make even a tiny bit of difference. Many of their jobs and personal lives are not very satisfying. Volunteering to serve others enriches their lives and often provides a new level of meaning and purpose for which they have been searching.

Resource Description

The corporation's employees, retirees, and occasionally their family members and friends can be used by the corporation to provide service to various segments of the community and its organizations. If the employees are given time off from their jobs to provide this service ("released time"), the contribution is technically the corporation's gift to the community. If the employees provide the service on their own time away from work, the contribution technically comes from the volunteers.

Corporations can provide informal assistance to community organizations by occasionally fulfilling requests to use some of their human resources on special assignments, or they can provide formal assistance. A formal, ongoing effort is called "corporate volunteerism." A corporate volunteer program results from the combined efforts of a corporation and individuals affiliated with that corporation who join forces to provide volunteer service to the community. The effort is initiated and sponsored by the corporation, which organizes, mobilizes, and manages the effort on behalf of the corporation as well as the volunteers.

Human resources channeled to the community include each employee and retiree participant's time; expertise; talents; commitment; dedication; connections; clout; ability to make corporate material resources available; ability to raise funds from inside and outside of the corporation; and often, but not necessarily, the ability to make personal financial contributions.

Benefits of Corporate Volunteer Programs

The corporation receives

1. A well-organized, orchestrated, and managed extension of its resources to provide needed services to the communities in which it operates through volunteerism
2. A positive boost in morale within its organization stemming from the revitalization, enthusiasm, and commitment that are experienced by those who volunteer
3. Gratitude to the corporation from the corporation's participants for sponsoring the volunteer program and enabling them to develop their skills, self-confidence, and values through volunteerism
4. Gratitude to the corporation from the corporation's community recipients for providing needed volunteer services

The volunteers receive

1. Opportunities to make a difference in the lives of others by sharing their time, talents, and expertise as volunteers through the corporation's program
2. Opportunities to meet new people and have new and varied experiences
3. Opportunities for leadership development and growth
4. Opportunities to develop team skills and to learn how to work with people
5. Opportunities to share their exciting and meaningful volunteer experiences with their relatives and friends

The community's agencies and schools receive

1. Opportunities to obtain needed assistance from the corporation's helping hands and leadership
2. Opportunities to accomplish their objectives and leverage their resources through the volunteers' assistance.

Source of the Corporate Resource

Corporate

Examples of corporate resources that come directly from a corporation or business are funds, staff, administrative operations, in-kind services, and employees who are granted released time from work.

Employees and Retirees

Examples of corporate resources that come indirectly from a corporation through the direct contribution of its employees and retirees are personal financial contributions and volunteer time.

Examples of Corporate Human Resources

1. Giving speeches or providing tours of corporate facilities
2. Serving as resource people on committees
3. Volunteering to help schools
4. Allowing employees who are parents to become involved in their children's schools
5. Obtaining pledges from coworkers for the employee's participation in a walkathon or fundraising event

Pros—Corporations

1. Corporations are teeming with employees and retirees who would like to become involved in their communities if only they knew how and were encouraged to do so.
2. When employees and retirees become involved in their communities on their corporation's behalf, an increase in their morale and loyalty to the corporation often results.

3. Corporate human resources are a positive supplement to limited corporate financial resources that are available to the community.

4. Corporate human resources provide talent, expertise, and helping hands that community organizations cannot afford to hire.

5. Assuming that the employees and retirees provide quality service to the community, the corporation receives excellent and positive public relations from the recipients of the community service, often resulting in new customers for the corporation.

Cons—Corporations

1. There may be an actual or perceived loss of productivity from participating employees, which makes released time a shrinking commodity as companies downsize. Released time also places more demands on a company's supervisors, who must maximize employee efficiency and output to compensate for an employee's release from work to do community service.

2. For corporations that have policies against employee solicitation of other employees on company premises during work hours, allowing employees to raise funds on an outside organization's behalf may create conflicts between policy and practice.

3. Liability issues apply whenever employees give information or provide service to people and organizations outside of the corporation. Corporate attorneys and risk management experts should be consulted to adequately and properly protect the corporation and its employees and retirees who participate in the community on the corporation's behalf.

4. Liability issues also apply regarding accident and injury claims by employees, retirees, and their relatives and friends who participate in community service on the corporation's behalf. Corporate attorneys and risk management experts should be consulted to protect the corporation.

5. Some employees have a difficult time keeping their priorities in order regarding their employment and their volunteer activities, especially those done on behalf of the corporation. Occasionally, some employ-

ees become more involved in and committed to their community service than to their jobs.

Pros—Schools

1. Schools receive extra helping hands at no cost.
2. New ideas and expertise from a corporate perspective provide opportunities to approach challenges and problems in a different manner.
3. Broad-based positive relationships with corporations may result.
4. Schools may gain entrée to corporations for resources in addition to corporate volunteers.
5. The availability of corporate volunteers enables schools to expand their goals and dreams.

Cons—Schools

1. Use of corporate volunteers may create a need for additional administration from the school, translating into cost.
2. Corporations may expect to become participants in some of the decision making applicable to the use of their volunteers.
3. Corporations may want or expect the schools to change or become more flexible in their operations in order to use the corporate volunteers.
4. Some corporations may expect the schools to accept all of the liability and risk that results from the corporate volunteers helping the schools.
5. Occasionally, some of the corporate volunteers may behave inappropriately or in a damaging manner to the school's property or people.

7

Corporate Resource No. 3: Influence

Sample Challenge

The superintendent of the school district in a major metropolitan area believes that a state assembly bill currently under consideration will, if passed, severely damage his and all other school districts in the state. He intends to do his own lobbying; however, he believes that his voice will not be heard above the voices of those who favor the bill, especially those from the business community.

Possible Outreach Solution

The superintendent knows that the influence of the CEO of the city's (and the state's) largest corporate employer will be heard much more loudly than his own. The superintendent could invite the CEO of that corporation to a private lunch to discuss the school district's views on the bill and how, if passed, it would negatively affect the district and therefore the community in which the corporation operates. If successful in persuading the CEO to agree with his position, the superintendent could ask the CEO to use his or her personal and corporate resources, such as the corporation's political action committee (PAC) and the corporation's state lobbyists, to actively try to defeat the bill.

Influence = Power

Politics is a fact of life in every arena of society. Some people and organizations recognize this reality and learn to work within the necessary systems to accomplish their goals, objectives, and dreams. Others refuse to play the game and are often defeated or hurt in the process. The ability to understand and use power and influence appropriately, respectfully, and wisely is a desirable skill to develop and hone for any representative of any institution. Like it or not, the degree of one's influence depends on variables such as whom you know, who you are, what you know, where you went to school, whom you represent, your title and position, and what you own.

Resource Description

Many corporations wield significant influence in the community because of their economic impact, the number of jobs they provide to residents, and their community involvement. By nature of being employed by or retired from these influential corporations, employees and retirees, especially high-ranking members of management, extend the corporation's influence when they lend assistance to the community either as corporate representatives or as private individuals.

It is often in the best interest of educational institutions to become involved with corporations that are perceived positively within the community and whose purposes and goals are closely aligned with their own. Influence can be employed through a variety of methods including writing, speaking, lobbying, contributing, supporting, and personally visiting.

Source of the Corporate Resource

Corporate

Examples of corporate resources that come directly from a corporation are funds, staff, administrative operations, corporate name and logo, support, and employees who are granted released time from work.

Employees and Retirees

Examples of corporate resources that come indirectly from a corporation through its employees and retirees are volunteer time outside of work hours, and support.

Examples of Influence

1. Lending the corporation's name to a list of supporters of a cause or to an organization that has purposes and goals that are compatible with the corporation's own purposes and goals
2. Allowing a member of corporate senior management to make an important speech or request something on behalf of an educational institution
3. Allowing a corporate employee with pertinent clout and expertise to testify or make proposals before local, state, and national hearings in support of an educational issue, institution, or coalition
4. Corporate lobbying for bills that support education's purposes and goals
5. Using a senior-level corporate executive as a chairperson or co-chairperson of an educational institution's event

Pros—Corporations

1. Influential involvement can be relatively cost free unless a monetary contribution is required in addition to the desired influential support.

2. Lending corporate influence can require minimal corporate staff time if the school agrees to provide all necessary staff support, including research and speech preparation assistance.

3. More than likely, the effort required by the corporation's influential involvement will be short term. However, that effort will go a long way in obtaining the support and goodwill of the educational institution being helped.

4. Good visibility and media coverage for the corporation as well as the school may result.

5. The corporation can be highly selective regarding how it chooses to lend its influential powers. It can do so by aligning itself with issues as well as educational institutions with philosophies and purposes similar to its own.

Cons—Corporations

1. The corporation must be cautious to ensure that its representatives clear all uses of corporate influence through a central corporate approval point; otherwise, corporate influence may be inadvertently lent to organizations whose purposes and intentions are in philosophical conflict with the corporation.

2. It may be difficult for the corporation to maintain control over how and when its name and influence are used.

3. Poor quality of staff support and follow-through committed to the corporation by the school could make the corporation and its representatives look bad, disorganized, and unprofessional.

4. Ill will and hostility could arise from people and organizations who are against the school that the corporation has chosen to support, thus resulting in a backlash of unwanted political negativism.

5. Wise and successful use of corporate influence requires advice from one or more corporate staff members with opinions and understandings of the community that are objective, comprehensive, and accurate. Such qualified staff members may not exist within the corporation. The corporation may not be comfortable with the idea of looking externally for such sensitive advice.

Pros—Schools

1. Unless the corporation has a largely negative public image, corporate influence is often stronger and more successful than the school's influence.
2. Success at requesting that a corporation use its influence on behalf of a school will, if not abused, go a long way toward cultivating an ongoing relationship between the corporation and the school.
3. Positive, powerful corporate influence can be very valuable.
4. There is no material cost of corporate influence.
5. Partnerships and coalitions are more powerful and can be far more successful than the efforts of a single individual, group, or institution.

Cons—Schools

1. The nonmaterial cost of using corporate influence on a school's behalf may be extremely high and may be carried over for an inordinately long period of time.
2. It is often difficult to disentangle oneself or an institution from a relationship when it is no longer beneficial.
3. Within the school, far too much time and effort could be required to receive the necessary approvals prior to asking a corporation to use its influence on the school's behalf.
4. A school may not have anyone of the required stature necessary to secure corporate influence.
5. There may not be a corporation with views that agree with and support those of the school or its school district.

8

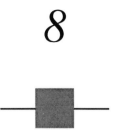

Corporate Resource No. 4: Information

Sample Challenge

A high school social studies teacher wants to develop an additional special unit on economics by focusing on the economic factors affecting the region in which the school is located. Because her major was English, she does not feel confident enough to develop the unit without lots of outside resources. It is especially important to the teacher that the information be real and directly applicable to the lives of her students and their families.

Possible Outreach Solution

The teacher can contact the economics departments of the major banks headquartered in the region and ask each of them to send her a copy of any regional economic information available through or published by the banks.

Information as a Commodity

We are living in the Information Age. The present and future success of institutions of all kinds, be they for profit or not for profit (such as schools), depends on information of all kinds (e.g., economic, demographic, historic, and future through forecasting). This kind of information is often obtained, used, and published by major corporations in departments with names like research, marketing, futures, and economics. Many of these departments make this information available to their clients and communities as a service at no cost or for fees.

Resource Description

Many corporations have access to or produce industry, corporate, economic, and other types of information that can be very useful to community and nonprofit organizations, such as schools, that do not have the ability or resources to produce or access this type of information on their own. By sharing this information, the corporation can make a significant and positive impact on the community.

Source of the Corporate Resource

Corporate

Examples of corporate resources that come directly from a corporation are funds, staff, administrative operations, information, data, databases, business systems, libraries, and employees who are granted released time from work.

Employees and Retirees

An example of a corporate resource that comes indirectly from a corporation through its employees and retirees is volunteer time outside of work hours.

Examples of Information

1. The information known and produced by a corporate economics department
2. The information available in a corporate library
3. Corporate publications based on original corporate research
4. Databases and management information systems used by a corporation
5. Original and standard business management systems used by the corporation

Pros—Corporations

1. Sharing information is an effective use of corporate resources already on hand.
2. Allowing schools to use a corporation's information is cost effective, especially if the information is already available to, compatible with, and easily transferable to the schools.
3. The information shared with schools may help spread a desired industry or corporate message and philosophy.
4. The information shared could be an effective and positive change agent for some aspect of the community.
5. Excellent public relations and positive media coverage may result for the corporation and the schools that use the information.

Cons—Corporations

1. The corporate information and systems may not be compatible with what the school can use, and to make it compatible could be too costly.
2. There is no way of knowing if the corporation's information will ever actually be used by a school or just put in a drawer or on a shelf because the school will not take the necessary time, does not have the needed ability or understanding, or does not possess the interest and desire to use the information.

3. There is a potential high cost of staff time required to make the information available.

4. Putting the corporate information into a format that can be easily used by a school could be very costly (e.g., typesetting, printing, using computer equipment and supplies, and providing staff time and expertise required to make necessary conversions).

5. The information shared might be misinterpreted, misused, or taken out of context, thus creating an effect opposite from the one the corporation intended.

Pros—Schools

1. Many schools cannot afford to purchase the latest information.

2. It is very costly for schools to conduct research and produce reports on information that is already available from outside sources.

3. Because most schools have limited resources and tight budgets, even if schools could conduct similar research to produce the desired information, duplication of effort is a waste of time and money.

4. Schools can better spend their human and material resources on their purposes for existence.

5. Availability of and access to needed information is a plus for any school.

Cons—Schools

There are none, as long as educators analyze the information for bias and use the information accordingly.

9

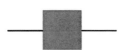

Corporate Resource No. 5:
In-Kind Contributions

Sample Challenge

A school district's job skills training program has decided to add a course called Supermarket Check-Out Clerk. The school board wants the classroom environment to be like an actual supermarket. Although the board has allocated a classroom and a teacher to the class, there are no additional funds for equipment and supplies.

Possible Outreach Solution

The administrator of the training program can approach the executive director of the foundation of each supermarket chain located in the state and request donations of supermarket equipment and supplies that are not currently and will not be used by the companies.

In-Kind Services

"In-kind services" is jargon for contributions of a company's products, supplies, resources, and services. The company usually receives a receipt for the amount of the estimated value of the in-kind contribution for tax-reporting purposes.

Resource Description

In-kind services consist of the work time and expertise of a corporation's employees and its material resources. The material resources include the corporation's own products and services as well as the materials, supplies, and capital equipment it already owns. Many corporations choose to contribute in-kind services to community organizations, such as schools, rather than or in addition to making a financial contribution.

Source of the Corporate Resource

Corporate

Sources of in-kind services are described above.

Examples of In-Kind Services

1. An airline company contributes a dozen round-trip tickets to the national conference of a national educators' association. The company also contributes two round-trip tickets anywhere in the continental United States for a door prize.
2. A corporation prints the invitations and programs for a school's annual fundraiser. The printing is done in the corporation's in-house print shop.
3. A major bank closes down one of its branch offices. It contributes all of the office furniture and teller windows from that branch to the local high school's Bank Teller class.

4. An advertising agency allows its staff to work on company time to design and provide camera-ready artwork for the local school volunteer program's annual service recognition celebration.

5. The corporate training department reserves a designated number of free registrations per class for school district administrators.

Pros—Corporations

1. In-kind services are usually cost effective because they do not require additional budget expenditures.

2. In-kind services are an excellent way to use remaining or phased-out corporate products and capital resources.

3. Publicity is usually provided by the educational institution by thanking, in print or in public, the corporation for its contribution.

4. Providing in-kind services performed by corporate employees is an efficient use of corporate staff time, especially during slow business periods.

5. Advertising results if the corporation's name and logo are printed on the in-kind products it contributes.

Cons—Corporations

1. Without a centralized system to track the contribution of in-kind services within the corporation, the corporation receives no credit for its contributions for tax and reporting purposes.

2. Not everyone or every organization will be happy with the corporation's choices of recipients of in-kind services. It is difficult for a corporation to decide which schools should receive in-kind contributions and which ones should not. The solution requires channeling additional corporate resources into a staff person or committee to coordinate the disbursement effort and create necessary guidelines and administrative procedures.

3. Without proper attention and controls, employees could easily misuse and abuse the donation of in-kind services, using in-kind contributions for personal gain.

4. Contributing in-kind services may be perceived as a waste of corporate resources by senior management and shareholders.

5. For a variety of reasons, the corporation may or may not want to receive public credit for in-kind contributions. Staff time and effort would be required to ensure that the desirable outcome of receiving or not receiving credit is achieved.

Pros—Schools

1. In-kind donations enable schools to stretch their budgets.
2. In-kind donations enable schools to extend their services.
3. Donated equipment is often more up to date than equipment on hand.
4. Donated expertise is professional and current.
5. If a school has access to donated expertise, such as legal or graphic arts services, the school will not have to add staff or hire consultants in these areas.

Cons—Schools

1. There may be transportation, delivery, and installation charges.
2. Storage problems may result if the donations are very large or numerous, and if they must be received only at times when the school is either unable to use them or has no storage space.
3. Used equipment must often be repaired before it can be used by the school.
4. Maintenance costs and contracts may cost more than the cost of new equipment.
5. Parts may no longer be available to maintain the donated equipment or products.

10

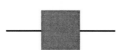

Corporate Resource No. 6: Leadership

Sample Challenge

Based on recent demographic studies, the director of institutional advancement of a large, multicultural metropolitan state university needs to expand and broaden the experience and backgrounds of his foundation's board of directors in order to represent the community from which the university's students and staff members are currently drawn.

Possible Outreach Solution

The director can reach out to executives from small, medium, and large businesses in the area to fill board positions, ensuring representative diversity and necessary management and leadership skills.

Corporate Leadership

It has been said that leadership is the ability to persuade others to seek defined objectives enthusiastically. It is the human factor that binds a group together and motivates it toward goals.

Corporate employees and retirees who volunteer to share their leadership experience and skills with external organizations satisfy their own needs for leadership participation, growth, and involvement in their community. Through their volunteer leadership experiences, corporate representatives are able to meet new people; have new, varied, and interesting experiences; develop new skills; and make a difference in the lives of others.

Corporate volunteer leaders are provided with a variety of experiences through which they can

1. Practice leadership
2. Learn how to work well with and through people who have different personalities, temperaments, backgrounds, and motivations
3. Learn how to delegate
4. Learn how to follow through
5. Learn how to apply procedures and practices to accomplish group goals

For every leader, regardless of the level of experience, leadership is a maturing process that benefits the leaders in every aspect of their lives and becomes a strong asset throughout their careers.

Resource Description

All levels of public and private schools can benefit greatly from the ideas and experiences of corporate leaders who have built their careers, cultivated their talent, and developed their leadership experience in challenging, ever-changing, competitive, and often international environments. Often, executives are seeking volunteer leadership positions in the community to fulfill personal, career, and corporate goals.

Source of the Corporate Resource

Corporate

As a corporate resource, leadership comes through the efforts of a corporation's management, supervisors, and employees who are granted released time from work. High-level executives do not actually have volunteer time of their own because many of them give nearly every waking hour to their corporations through their business and community involvements. This type of dedication "comes with the territory" for top management, and middle managers often give as much in their quest to move up the corporate ladder.

Employees and Retirees

Many employees who cannot take time off from the job gladly contribute their own time to participate as leaders within the community. Many retirees want to be able to share their knowledge and experience and remain connected to community life.

Examples of Corporate Leadership

1. Corporate executives serve on nonprofit and school boards, often in officer or leadership positions.
2. Senior corporate executives serve on blue ribbon advisory committees that assist school superintendents and high-level administrators in decision making.
3. Corporations loan executives and retirees to nonprofit organizations such as United Way and to school districts.
4. Corporate leaders serve as visiting lecturers in their areas of expertise at universities and community colleges.
5. Middle managers participate in Junior Achievement programs as teachers and advisers.

Pros—Corporations

1. Quality corporate leadership is gratefully received by the community organizations and schools.
2. The morale and self-satisfaction of corporate leaders and retirees are enhanced. Many of these people are revitalized and stimulated by sharing their leadership expertise and interacting with people from the community.
3. Community involvement provides excellent growth opportunities for middle managers; it also enables retirees to be active and share their knowledge and experience.
4. By sharing its leaders with the community, the corporation receives multiple opportunities to expand its level of influence externally.
5. External leadership opportunities enable corporate participants to interface with peers from the private and public sectors, creating opportunities for developing new business and bringing external ideas back into the corporation for stimulation, comparison, and consideration.

Cons—Corporations

1. While the corporate leaders are away providing service to the community, there is a loss of productivity during the regular workday, which can be very costly at senior levels.
2. A corporation must be careful to select community organizations and schools with philosophies, purposes, and goals that are supportive of and compatible with the corporation's own purposes and goals; otherwise, the service efforts may be counterproductive and even embarrassing to the corporation.
3. If the corporation decides it wants to monitor and count the hours of community service of its leaders, this administrative process is time consuming and must be centrally managed to be effective.
4. Often, corporate leaders are expected to provide to the community organizations and schools they serve not only their personal leader-

ship but also their corporate and sometimes even their own personal financial contributions.

5. Liability is a major concern for both the corporation and the participating corporate leaders. Corporations must provide adequate legal advice and insurance to protect the corporation and each corporate leader who is acting on the corporation's behalf within the community.

Pros—Schools

1. Representatives of a school district's administrative team have the benefit of business skills, experience, and counsel without having to pay for them.
2. Using outside corporate leadership enhances the institution's reputation.
3. Strong boards and advisory committees that consist in part of corporate leaders can enhance a school's fund and resource development opportunities.
4. Using high-level corporate leaders for presentations at hearings strengthens an educational institution's position on pending political matters and bills.
5. Having good working relationships with business leaders can open doors for additional benefits and resources.

Cons—Schools

1. Most high-level corporate leaders often come with big egos that must be catered to.
2. Corporate executives have very tight calendars and require that each minute of their time be wisely and effectively used.
3. Sometimes, to secure the use of a very senior-level corporate executive on an advisory committee or an educational foundation, the school must accept being able to use the corporate executive's name and title, and then work on a day-to-day basis with one or more junior

executives delegated to the task of representing him or her in the community.

4. Occasionally, the school must plan its schedules around the availability of high-level corporate executives.

5. Chief executive officers and other members of top corporate management often have bodyguards and other assistants whose needs must be met.

11

Corporate Resource No. 7:
Mandatory Involvement

Resource Description

Situations can arise from outside as well as inside a corporation that require the corporation to become involved in the community in very specific ways. In these situations, people and organizations have the power to demand the corporation's involvement. The corporation must respond satisfactorily to an external mandate or face fines, restrictions, and/or sanctions.

Outreach Opportunity

If a corporation is publicly held or licensed, such as a bank or television station, the law states that such corporations must be involved in or support the community. It is in the best interest of educational institutions to become aware of the corporations within their communities that have to meet these kinds of requirements and "get in line" to receive the benefits.

The information provided in Part II of this book outlining the 12 corporate resources also applies in cases of mandated involvement. Schools will be able to benefit best from the opportunities resulting from mandated corporate involvement by doing their homework and discovering how best to capitalize on each unique mandate affecting a corporation.

Source of the Corporate Resource

Examples of corporate resources that can be made available to schools because of mandated involvement are funds, staff, administrative operations, and employees who are granted released time from work.

Examples of Mandated Involvement

1. The financial industry is governed by a U.S. law called the Financial Institutions Reform, Recovery and Enforcement Act, which mandates that financial institutions serve all of the citizens who reside within the communities in which the institutions operate.
2. A corporation's CEO decides that the corporation will contribute $1 million to fight the war on drugs.
3. U.S. affirmative action laws have mandated that corporations must hire fairly and equally from their communities.
4. A senior-level executive pledges $50,000 of corporate funds to his alma mater over a 5-year period.
5. A corporation is found guilty of misconduct by the courts and ordered to contribute $1 million to its community along with 100,000 hours of community service that must be performed by members of the corporation's senior management.

Pros—Corporations

1. Usually, the net result of mandated involvement is that good deeds are performed in the community through the corporation's efforts regardless of whether or not they are performed voluntarily.

2. Employees assigned to implement mandated actions learn about the needs of the community and its institutions, including schools. Many of these employees continue to be involved in the community throughout their careers and after they retire because they have developed the sincere commitment to community need.

3. Federally mandated community involvement requires corporations to channel staff and budget into the effort. Once established, these internal operational structures, often very efficient and effective, can be used by the corporation to expand community involvement beyond what is mandated.

4. Excellent public relations and positive media coverage may result for the corporation from internally mandated community involvement.

5. Skilled media experts often can generate positive public relations and media coverage from externally mandated community involvement, thus creating favorable public opinion of the corporation from potentially negative situations.

Cons—Corporations

1. Mandated and unplanned community involvement and resulting budget expenditures can throw a strategic plan off course and force changes in existing community relations plans. These changes cause great frustration for the managers who must manage these challenging situations to positive conclusions.

2. To have a balanced year-end budget, funds must be cut or scaled down from other preplanned budget categories and financial commitments to community organizations.

3. The mandates create resentment in managers who must work miracles to end the year on or under budget.

4. Negative employee opinion is generated if the corporation's employees have not been adequately prepared to participate in the mandated community involvement. The problem intensifies if the story receives negative publicity either internally or externally.

5. Senior management and shareholders may be angered by what they perceive as emotional decision making or poor business decisions that may have been responsible for drawing the attention of the mandating organization to their corporation's operations.

Pros—Schools

A school can benefit in numerous ways if the corporation's mandate enables the corporation to support or become involved with that particular kind of institution.

Cons—Schools

1. Corporate involvement will be spelled out by each particular mandate.
2. A corporation may be willing to go only as far as the mandate requires.
3. A particular mandate may preclude certain types of nonprofit institutions, such as schools.
4. The spirit in which the corporate "gift" is given may be clouded by the fact that the gift is not being given by choice.
5. There may be some negative public relations consequences that result from a school being the recipient of resources from a corporation in trouble.

12

Corporate Resource No. 8: Money

Sample Challenge

The band teacher in a middle school wants to buy uniforms for the advanced band. She needs several thousand dollars and has been told by the principal that no funds can be made available for this purchase.

Possible Outreach Solution

The band teacher can approach the corporation that adopted her school and ask the corporation to provide the uniforms.

Money, Money, Money, Money

There's only one thing wrong with money. There's never enough of it. This same problem applies to corporations, nonprofit organizations, schools, and individuals. In any economy, but especially in a slow economy, additional financial pressures present themselves.

Although the outcome that the band teacher wants in the above solution could happen because of the adoption relationship between the school and the corporation, a positive outcome would be highly unlikely in normal circumstances. That is why it is important to remember that corporations have many other kinds of resources, as explained in detail throughout this book. If a school is unsuccessful at receiving money from a corporation, the school should look at some of the other nonmonetary resource options before giving up entirely on that corporation.

Personal Relationships

Most monetary contributions received by a school from a corporation come because of a strong personal relationship between a corporate representative and a school representative that is perceived by the corporation as important. That type of a relationship can be cultivated by following the ideas presented in chapter 2, "Acquiring Savvy for the Corporate Experience," and then working creatively and persistently with the chapter's concepts until strong, mutually beneficial, ongoing relationships are cultivated between the school and the corporation.

Grantsmanship

Many schools decide to go after monetary grants from corporate foundations. This decision pushes those schools into a new world requiring very specific knowledge and skills that many people wrap up into a new profession called grantwriter. Being a good writer is just one of those necessary skills. Two excellent suggestions for succeeding in the arena of corporate grants are (a) follow the suggestions recommended in chapter 2; and (b) read and study everything you can get your hands on about grantwriting, and be sure to take a first-class, in-depth seminar in grantwriting from an instructor and an organization of the caliber of the Grantsmanship Center, located in Los Angeles, which presents numerous seminars throughout the year in many cities. Your school must consider the cost of your education and training in grantsmanship as mandatory and critical to its financial success!

There is such keen competition in the grant world that taking a seminar and continuing to hone the grantwriting skills of those who are writing grants should become a top priority for any educational institution that decides to compete for grants.

Here are the basics:

1. Research the corporate foundations that have expressed and demonstrated an interest in contributing to organizations with a mission and purpose such as your school's.

2. Request a copy of their grant guidelines and most recent annual report.

3. Read and study every word to determine if your school qualifies according to each foundation's specific requirements and expressed contribution interests.

4. If your school and project qualify, follow every single word of instructions regarding the preparation and mailing of your grant application.

5. Mail your application. Then don't hold your breath, count your chickens, or sit and wait for the money to arrive. Move on to other applications and school activities that will help your school meet its needs and goals for financial assistance.

6. If you are awarded the grant, be sure that your school and its program fulfill all of their obligations and commitments and achieve all of their goals to the highest degree possible. Using the foundation's money to its satisfaction will help your school win future grants because foundations like to give their money to organizations that have demonstrated their vision and their ability to achieve their goals and use donated funds effectively.

Resource Description

Many corporations make financial contributions to schools. Some corporations pledge contributions based on a certain percentage of pre- or post-tax earnings. The methods of distributing these financial contributions vary from corporation to corporation depending on the size of the corporation, its contributions budget, and its contributions guidelines.

Source of the Corporate Resource

Corporate money comes from a corporation's earnings, hopefully profits, that a corporation allocates to one or more of the following budgets:
operational, contributions, or foundation.

Examples of How Corporate
Contributions Are Made

1. A corporation establishes a separate nonprofit foundation through
   which it distributes its contributions to the community.
2. Funds are distributed to the community by a contributions department of the corporation.
3. Corporate contributions are decentralized, with representatives of
   local management placing the funds where they believe the funds
   will do the most good.
4. The corporation establishes a matching gifts program for its employees and retirees through which the amount of the employee's or
   retiree's own personal contribution to his or her chosen community
   or nonprofit organization or school is matched at a specified percentage by the corporation.
5. The corporation establishes local community service committees
   composed of a desired mix of individuals such as local corporate
   management; employees representing all corporate levels, ages, and
   ethnic backgrounds; and retirees. The purpose of these committees is
   to distribute corporate contributions to community and nonprofit
   organizations and schools based on each committee's evaluation of
   community needs and the corporation's own established goals for the
   committees.

Pros—Corporations

1. Often, the gift of money is all that is desired by the community
   organization or school that receives a contribution or grant; therefore,
   little or no follow-up is required from the corporation, minimizing
   staff time.

2. Tax advantages exist for corporate contributions.

3. Staff requirements often can be kept relatively small for corporate contributions.

4. Excellent public relations and positive media coverage may result from corporate contributions if made public.

5. The corporation is responding to true and serious community needs by making financial contributions to community and nonprofit organizations and schools.

Cons—Corporations

1. There is never enough money to satisfy all of the community needs expressed through seemingly endless grant requests.

2. The establishment of a separate nonprofit foundation to handle corporate contributions can be a very costly and involved process that results in a more restrictive vehicle for giving money to the community than through a corporate contributions department.

3. The more decentralized the corporate contributions effort, the more difficult it becomes to maintain consistent standards of giving and ensure complete contribution records for financial, reporting, and tax purposes.

4. Many large corporations operate a variety of contributions vehicles, thus increasing the complexity and difficulty of maintaining consistent giving standards and accurate records.

5. It is often very difficult to develop a contributions budget plan for the following year when actual available funds depend on the financial health of the corporation during that same budget year. Add to this uncertainty those contributions commitments that have been made over a multiple-year period and the internally mandated and unbudgeted pledges, and many contributions managers grow very frustrated trying to satisfy too many requests and demands with insufficient financial resources.

Pros—Schools

Financial gifts can be used to purchase the items and fund the projects desired.

Cons—Schools

1. There is not enough money to go around, and competition for corporate contributions and grants is very stiff.
2. Grantwriting is very time consuming with uncertain returns.
3. Usually, corporations cannot fund operational costs.
4. Strings may be attached to the grant.
5. The grant probably will be a one-time or 1-year gift, leaving the school facing the same funding problems in the future.

13

Corporate Resource No. 9: Material Resources

Sample Challenge

The principal of a middle school located in the inner city needs a place to hold the annual volunteer tutor recognition breakfast. The volunteers have expressed the fact that they are tired of the local hotel where previous events have been held.

Possible Outreach Solution

Because the son of the chairman of the board of the local insurance company sits on the school district's school board, the district superintendent decides to help the principal by seeing if the chairman would be willing to host the recognition breakfast in the company's executive dining room at no cost to the school or the volunteers.

Materials: The Most Creative Resource

Corporate money is tight. The availability of corporate human resources is limited because of job demands. Fortunately, a corporation's material possessions are an untapped resource for schools. Sharing corporate material resources with community groups enables schools to stretch their budgets while helping corporations accomplish some of their community service goals.

Resource Description

Corporations have material resources that can be very beneficial to community/nonprofit organizations and schools if these groups are allowed to use them. Although the corporation must use some of these resources in its daily business operations, there are times when the resources can be made available for use by community organizations and schools.

Examples of Corporate Material Resources

1. Teaching high school students entry-level jobs on corporate premises, using corporate equipment, supplies, and employees as teachers; instruction occurs during evenings and weekends or when a corporation is not using the facilities
2. Hosting a school's annual fundraiser in a corporation's executive dining room
3. Allowing an art program from a nearby school to exhibit its best works in a corporation's lobby
4. Allowing a school to use a corporation's training rooms for staff development
5. Providing training on corporate computers for employees from schools and community or nonprofit organizations

Pros—Corporations

1. A corporation is able to maximize the use of its material resources, help the community, and receive excellent public relations and positive media coverage.

2. Many community and nonprofit organizations and school districts provide "hold harmless" insurance protection for corporations when corporations allow them to use corporate premises, material, and human resources.

3. Corporate employees are required to supervise the use of a corporation's material resources when they are being used by community and nonprofit organizations and schools. Because of the hands-on involvement of a corporation's supervisors, this supervision stimulates and encourages more corporate employees to become further involved in the community.

4. Few additional corporate expenditures are incurred beyond the use of the material resources, especially if a corporation owns its own buildings and is not a tenant who must pay for utilities after normal work hours.

5. A corporation can receive excellent positive public relations.

Cons—Corporations

1. Corporate coordination and additional staff may be required to oversee the use of corporate material resources by external people and groups.

2. Liability issues must be adequately addressed and proper protection arranged by a corporation's risk management experts whenever external people come onto corporate premises.

3. Confidential issues must be adequately addressed and procedures developed regarding corporate databases and confidential files that might be accessed by external people, such as teachers and students, either accidentally or intentionally.

4. Precautions must be taken regarding possible theft of and damage to corporate employees' personal property as well as to corporate property.

5. Staff time is required to develop guidelines, criteria, and operational procedures to determine which external groups can use and which cannot use the material resources and how that use shall occur.

Pros—Schools

1. School employees have access and are exposed to state-of-the-art equipment and technology that their school cannot afford, thus

enabling a school's employees to keep abreast of current technology and business trends.

2. School employees can learn the latest management and business procedures from their corporate peers.

3. Use of corporate material resources stretches school budgets.

4. Use of corporate material resources removes some of the barriers that separate the for-profit from the not-for-profit worlds.

5. Ongoing use of corporate material resources by schools cultivates close working relationships between the staff members of each organization.

Cons—Schools

1. Dealing with corporate red tape may be frustrating to school staff members.

2. The cost to schools of insurance and risk management may not be worth the amount saved by being able to use corporate resources.

3. A school may not feel comfortable always being on the receiving end of a corporate relationship.

4. A school may not want the burden of being responsible for corporate resources that are loaned rather than given.

5. A corporation may ask for favors in return.

14

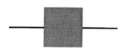

Corporate Resource No. 10: Partnerships

Sample Challenge

The superintendent of a school district wants to upgrade the quality and usefulness of the district's vocational classes to the students as well as to the future employers who will hire them.

Possible Outreach Solution

The superintendent can create a community classroom division based on the formation of partnerships with local businesses and industries. The school district can provide the advertising for the classes, the recruitment of the students, the students, the staff coordinators, an hourly rate of pay for the corporate staff members who become the teachers, the processing of documentation for the corporate teachers to acquire vocational designated-subject

teaching credentials, the school credit for the students, and the insurance to
hold the corporations harmless.

The corporation can provide use of its facilities as community classrooms, corporate equipment, class materials, and qualified staff to serve as
teachers, at no cost to the school.

Public-Private Partnerships

In the 1980s and 1990s, the establishment of partnerships has played a
role in national school reform as well as community improvement through
public/private partnerships. In fact, in the educational arena, the word *partnership* has become jargon referring to any relationship between a school and
a business.

Resource Description

Business/school partnerships can be similar in form to many of the other
11 corporate resources discussed throughout Part II of this book. The significant difference is that the corporate effort is conducted through a formal
partnership with one or more educational institutions and possibly one or
more nonprofit or community organizations and other corporations. Therefore, rather than being responsible for the entire effort through the contribution of corporate resources, the corporation is responsible only for a
preagreed-upon portion. Partnership involvement can vary from a single
event to a long-term, ongoing program or obligation.

Source of the Corporate Resource

Corporate

Partnerships use corporate resources such as funds, staff, administrative
operations, and employees who are granted released time from work.

Employees and Retirees

Corporate resources coming from a corporation's employees and retirees are in the form of their volunteer time outside of work hours.

Examples of Public-Private Partnerships

1. California's Regional Occupational Program (ROP), a job-training partnership that functions in the manner described in the solution in this chapter

2. Participation in a coalition of downtown corporations that join together to support inner-city schools, whereby each corporation agrees to provide some of its products to do the job (e.g., paint, equipment, window glass, plants and other greenery, sculptures, stonework, as well as a corps of its employee volunteers to do the work)

3. The WorkAbility program, in which a corporation agrees to hire and train handicapped students in a specific job for a prescribed length of time, and the WorkAbility program reimburses the corporation for the salary it pays the students and provides ongoing coordination and supervision by program staff

4. A community college's vocational program that recruits local corporations to commit to supporting a portion of the program (e.g., providing speakers on careers, teaching participants how to fill out employment applications, making financial contributions for clothing for students to go on job interviews, providing tours of the corporations, and contributing in-kind services for the college's day care program)

5. A partnership between a corporation and its employees who volunteer in schools (e.g., for every verified hour of service an employee contributes to a community organization on his or her own time, the corporation contributes a specified amount of money to that same school)

Pros—Corporations and Schools

1. Each institution is responsible only for a piece of a partnership effort rather than having to undertake the entire project or program by itself.

2. Partnerships are very good leverages of each organization's resources.

3. Partnerships between corporations and schools, government, and community organizations are in vogue. By being an active partner, an institution can be positioned as a leader in the national partnership movement; and strong, effective, active partnerships can be instrumental in enabling an institution's members to be awarded both federal and corporate grants.

4. An institution can select partners with which it wants to be affiliated.

5. Excellent public relations and positive media coverage may result.

Cons—Corporations and Schools

1. An organization has quality control only over its portion of the partnership.

2. Partnerships require staff time to coordinate properly.

3. As the partners and people change within a partnership, the strength and effectiveness of the partnership also changes.

4. In a partnership, each organization does not receive as much credit and recognition as if it operated its own unique program or project.

5. Partnership management can be very complex. Clear communication can be a challenge because of the number of managers and coordinators assigned to the partnership from each participating partner.

15

Corporate Resource No. 11:
Programs

Sample Challenge

The program coordinator of an adult education program for older adults wants to start a luncheon series with speakers on a variety of subjects that will be of interest and assistance to seniors.

Possible Outreach Solution

The coordinator can call several of the local corporations and see if any of them have speakers bureaus that provide speakers on a variety of subjects at no cost.

Resource Description

Corporations can research, design, implement, operate, and refine their own community relations programs that fit the corporation's culture, operations processes, leadership philosophy, assessment of community needs, and established priorities. Corporations also can participate in a school's program by providing the support requested.

Source of the Corporate Resource

Corporate

The sources of corporate resources that can be channeled into programs are funds, staff, administrative operations, and employees who are granted released time from work.

Employees and Retirees

As a result of a corporation's desire to help the community, employees and retirees can learn about opportunities to volunteer their time outside of work hours to help schools.

Examples of Corporate Programs

1. Employee and retiree volunteer programs
2. Speakers and tour bureaus
3. A matching gifts program for community organizations and schools selected by employees and retirees
4. A mentor program for potential high school dropouts
5. A minority purchasing program

Pros—Corporations

1. Participating employees and retirees often show an increase in morale and loyalty to the company.

2. A corporation is positioned as a creative, innovative, dedicated, socially responsible corporate citizen within the community when quality programs are showcased.

3. Quality corporate programs deliver excellent and needed service to schools.

4. Programs can be designed to address each of a corporation's major areas of community concern.

5. Quality programs promote a corporation as one that pays more than lip service to community need.

Cons—Corporations

1. Quality programs require top-notch staff, sufficient budgets, and sustained corporate effort for the programs to be effective.

2. Continued top management support is essential. It is difficult for programs to succeed when senior management changes its personnel, philosophy, and priorities.

3. Many programs are only as good as their current managers and coordinators.

4. If programs must be reduced or eliminated, a tremendous amount of unhappiness and dissatisfaction will be generated both internally, by employee and retiree participants, and externally, by the organizations that received the benefits, resulting in negative internal and external public relations as well as reduced services to the community.

5. Often, the survival of a program is determined by its connection with one senior-level executive or the CEO. If the supportive executive is no longer powerful within the corporation, the program's existence could be jeopardized. Therefore, much effort by community relations department staff members must go into the ongoing selling of each important program broadly across top management as the players change and new heirs apparent emerge. This sales effort requires much time and energy and could produce negative perceptions rather than producing the positive results desired and required.

Pros—Schools

Free use of

- Facilities
- Personnel
- Expertise
- Materials
- Supplies

Cons—Schools

1. The corporation may be the "driver" of the program, with the school's representatives and clients in the "back seat."
2. The corporation probably will require the school to provide insurance holding the corporation "harmless" in every instance except for negligence.
3. Some corporations may not be open to suggestions regarding program operation.
4. The school may be required to provide staff support in order to participate in the corporation's program.
5. The corporation's program may be held only during regular work hours, thus preventing some schools and their clients from participating.

16

Corporate Resource No. 12: Relationships

Sample Challenge

The superintendent of a school district has been sensing a lack of board support from some of the long-term members. At a recent reception held at the headquarters of the gas company, the superintendent noticed the president of his school board talking at great length with the senior vice president of community relations, who happens to be a close personal friend of the superintendent.

Possible Outreach Solution

Because of the excellent relationship the superintendent has maintained with his friend, both on a personal and professional basis, the superintendent may wish to discuss his work situation with his friend, in complete confidence, and see if he can ascertain any insight into his board president's views of the school district and the superintendent's role within it. The superintendent believes this information will enable him to develop a plan to improve his own personal performance and his effectiveness with his board.

Resource Description

In business, as with people, often it is not only what you know but also whom you know that can make the difference between success and failure in a situation. A key relationship, either strictly professional or strictly personal, can be beneficial to an educational institution, such as bringing in a new major donor, generating excellent community relations, ongoing fund development, recruiting new students, and filling positions on advisory committees with excellent people.

Many corporations and school districts encourage their executives and managers to cultivate key relationships in the community.

Source of the Corporate Resource

Corporate

The sources of relationships that are made possible because of a corporation's commitment to community involvement are the members of management and staff who are granted released time from work.

Employees and Retirees

Many corporations encourage their employees and retirees to become involved in the community through their volunteer time outside of work hours.

Examples of Corporate Relationships

1. Many corporations research key contacts who would be beneficial to the corporation and then develop a corporatewide strategy for cultivating relationships with them.

2. Many corporations encourage members of management to join community boards, clubs, committees, and organizations.

3. Corporations encourage managers and staff, especially those whose efforts contribute to the bottom line, to network at every opportunity at business, social, and community events. This effort is often called "business or practice development."

4. To achieve certain corporate goals, corporations target select groups with which to become involved (e.g., minority, service, business, nonprofit, and school organizations).

5. Good corporate citizens believe it is their responsibility to help people, groups, community organizations, and schools within the communities served by their corporations.

Pros—Corporations and Schools

1. In the beginning, only a little extra effort is required by representatives of an organization to cultivate useful relationships. Soon, the effort becomes second nature and is an ongoing process.

2. The organizational costs are minimal (e.g., meals, memberships, phone calls, released time away from the regular workday).

3. When organizations need help, a favorable relationship can lead to a desirable outcome by opening a door or providing direct assistance to resolve a situation.

4. Relationships have a multiplying factor, maximizing the initial investment of time, effort, and cost.

5. Relationships transcend organizational boundaries. For example, a new executive brings with him or her a network of established relationships that may prove useful to his or her new employer. Those relationships often benefit the organization even when the executive moves on in his or her career.

Cons—Corporations and Schools

1. Relationships are no stronger than the characters and personalities of the parties involved.

2. If a relationship has been abused or overused, it might not be beneficial to the organization when the organization really needs help.

3. Tides can turn. An individual who has developed a relationship with a particular representative of an organization may have learned something about him or her or the organization during the process. The individual could use this information against the organization's representative or the organization itself in the future.

4. If an employee feels pressured by his or her organization to develop relationships, he or she may be tempted to try to "buy" a relationship, thus setting the stage for future ethical and legal problems.

5. An organization's representative may not be able to judge the actual potential value of a relationship and therefore may put considerable time, effort, and money into building a powerless or negative relationship rather than a strong, positive relationship that could be helpful to the organization.

Appendixes

Appendix A:
Corporate and Foundation Resources Worksheet

Part I: Corporation or Foundation

Name: _____

Address: _____

City: _____ State: _____ Zip: _____

    Mailing Address (if different from above):

_____

City: _____ State: _____ Zip: _____

Chief Executive (CEO): _____

    Title: _____

    Phone: (_____)_____

Primary Contact: _____

    Title: _____

    Phone: (_____)_____

    Address (if different from above):

_____

City: _____ State: _____ Zip: _____

    Mailing Address (if different from above):

_____

City: _____ State: _____ Zip: _____

Part II: Resource Analysis

Resources available from this corporation	Has (X)	Could or might give to us? (Yes/No)	Plan for procuring (Notes)
Events			
Human resources			
Influence			
Information			
In-kind contributions			
Leadership			
Mandatory involvement			
Money			
Material resources			
Partnerships			
Programs			
Relationships			
Other			

Appendix B: Relationship Record

Date of Contact	Who (Us)	Contacted whom (Them)	Why?	Results

Appendix C: Contributions Record

Date	Gift/Value	From whom? (Them)	Purpose	Thank you from whom? (Us)/Date

CORWIN
PRESS

The Corwin Press logo—a raven striding across an open book—represents the happy union of courage and learning. We are a professional-level publisher of books and journals for K–12 educators, and we are committed to creating and providing resources that embody these qualities. Corwin's motto is "Success for All Learners."